IMPERIAL PALACES OF RUSSIA

IMPERIAL PALACES OF RUSSIA

PRINCE MICHAEL OF GREECE

PHOTOGRAPHS BY FRANCESCO VENTURI

Translated from the French
by Catherine O'Keeffe

Tauris Parke Books, London

For Olga

The author, photographer and publisher would like to thank the following for their help in the production of this book: Alexander Bartenev, the Italian Consul, Mr and Mrs De Martino, Anthony and Elizabeth Dymock, Andrei Maylunas, Gregory Melianenkov, Nicolai Obuchovich, George Orbely, Neil Pattenden, Lucas Praun, John Stuart, Gloria Venturi, Victoria Zhelnova, the curators of the Imperial palaces; and Celia, for the sunny days.

Special thanks to Valery Zhukov.

FRONTISPIECE At Oranienbaum, the eighteenth-century Italian fashion for classical ruins and figures is evident. This classical head, which occupies a sober corner of the Chinese Pavilion, is in fact a copy.

Published by Tauris Parke Books,
45 Bloomsbury Square, London WC1A 2HY
in association with KEA Publishing Services Ltd., London.

Text and captions © 1992 Prince Michael of Greece
Photographs © 1992 Francesco Venturi/KEA Publishing Services Ltd.

All rights reserved. No part or content of this book may be reproduced without the written permission of the Publisher.

The Cataloguing in Publication Data for this book is available from the British Library, London.

ISBN 1-85043-231-7

Typesetting by Spire Origination, Norwich
Colour separation by Amilcare Pizzi s.p.a., Milan, Italy
Printed by Amilcare Pizzi s.p.a., Milan, Italy

Contents

Detail of the front façade of the Skating Pavilion at Oranienbaum.

Introduction 7

The Summer Palace and Garden 13

Peterhof 21

The Winter Palace 39

Oranienbaum 47

Ropcha 58

The Marble Palace 61

Chesme 64

Tauride Palace 67

Tsarskoye Selo 73

Pavlovsk 89

Old Michael's Castle 112

Kamennostrovsky Palace 118

Yelagin Palace 123

Michael's Palace 127

Peterhof Cottage 131

The Winter Palace under Nicholas I and Alexander II 143

Strelna 154

Marinsky Palace 157

Grand Duke Nicholas' Palace 162

New Michael's Palace 166

Gatchina Palace 169

Anichkov Palace 183

Grand Duke Vladimir's Palace 189

Belosseilsky Belosievsky 193

Tsarskoye Selo and the Winter Palace under Nicholas II 201

Index 216

Introduction

NO court in the world has ever been more majestic, more sumptuous, more extravagant than the Russian Imperial Court, and it is still remembered as a scintillating legend. It had as its setting the most numerous, vast and luxurious palaces in the world. Colonnades stretched out for miles through the acres of parks which were liberally dotted with pavilions, each one more precious than the last. The gilded onion domes of the chapels surmounted the trophies and caryatids decorating the blue, pink and pistachio façades. Everything about these palaces was on a colossal scale: the greenhouses, the outbuildings, the stables, even the dolls' houses.

Inside, rare marbles, malachite, lapis lazuli, jasper, agate and amber were used, as if these were the commonest of building materials. Ivory and gilded bronze enhanced the rarest woods. In one room, Chinese plates were mounted into amber panels, in another literally priceless paintings were hung cheek by jowl. Catherine the Great bought entire collections of works of art from Western Europe and Nicholas I built the most magnificent museum to house these countless masterpieces. The tapestries, furniture, carpets and porcelain all came from the best workshops and factories. Gold, enamel and precious stones decorated the slightest trinket, such as those left by Fabergé, the last Tsar's goldsmith. This excessive display was intended to impress and dazzle, as befitted the seat of the greatest empire in the world, one created by centuries of bitter war against invaders from every side and convulsed by bloody upheavals. Russia possessed more territory than any nation in history, and in each area there were unimaginably abundant natural resources.

Everything in this vast nation revolved around one person, the Tsar, and around one city, St Petersburg. Moscow was nothing more than a memory, a rather unpleasant one at that, which was recalled only for coronations. It was in St Petersburg and its surroundings that everything was concentrated: the palaces, the country houses, the hunting lodges and the Imperial summer houses. Nearly all were designed by foreign architects, Italians for the most part: Antonio Rinaldi, Bartolommeo Rastrelli, Carlo Rossi, Giacomo Quarenghi; some Germans too, such as Andrei Stakenschneider. They served a dynasty which the extinction of the Romanov line has rendered foreign both physically and in spirit, in spite of their admirable intentions. They helped create the illusion that was St Petersburg by the marvellous creations they constructed in such unpromising surroundings. It became a privileged enclave, a fairy-tale world which cut its inhabitants off from reality, the Imperial family in particular. They gradually retreated to this region, only venturing out to cross the Empire for holidays in the Crimea, for rest cures in a Western spa or a visit to an English or German cousin.

Nicholas I's study at Peterhof Cottage (see page 131). The study is in the attic of the Cottage and is hung with neo-Gothic wallpaper. The furniture and the nocturnal sea scene are characteristic of Nicholas I's austere tastes and lack of interest in the arts.

My grandfather, George I, King of Greece, only just installed on his fragile throne, went in search of a wife. He found her in Russia, a beautiful young girl, barely fifteen, the Grand Duchess Olga Constantinovna. The links between the two families multiplied. My grandfather's sister married the successor to the throne, the future Alexander III. My father's two sisters married Grand Dukes, and one of his brothers, Nicholas, took as his second wife the beautiful Grand Duchess Elena Vladimirovna. My grandmother Olga never forgot her native country, to the extent that when their daughter, Alexandra, left to marry the Grand Duke Paul, my grandfather said to her: 'My daughter, I hope that you will remain as Greek in Russia as your mother has remained Russian in Greece.' My grandmother, having produced enough princes and princesses to consolidate the young and fragile Greek throne, managed to Russianize her youngest son, my father Christopher. He was born at the palace of Pavlovsk and each year she took him to Russia to stay with their innumerable relations. Years later, he could recall every detail of these fabulous trips:

The Imperial Court was the most magnificent of the European courts, to the extent that there was something barbarous about its splendour. Derived from ancient Byzantium, its ceremonies evoked the glorious times of Catherine the Great and of France during the eighteenth century. Money flowed and nothing was too expensive, even if it afforded only a moment's pleasure. The Emperor had at his disposal the abundant resources of a powerful empire and the Imperial family counted its revenue in millions. Copes were trimmed with ermine and sable, and harness buckles were made of gold and silver. The luxury industries flourished and artists and musicians gathered from all over the world, certain in the knowledge that they would find patrons. But below this brilliant surface, discontent crept silently in the shadows, like a stalking animal, only showing its head from time to time, up to the day when it finally pounced and completely reversed the entire social system.

Each Grand Duke had his own personal Court and coat of arms. The ladies-in-waiting attached to the Grand Duchesses wore costumes in the Court's colours. When they were all assembled for great occasions, such as Easter, Epiphany or the blessing of the waters, the effect they created was like a scene from the Middle Ages. The costumes shone with precious stones whose value could be counted in millions of pounds, worn with necklaces whose diamonds were so big that they look unreal, and rubies and emeralds as big as pigeons's eggs mounted in traditional tiaras. Each branch of the family had its own collection of historical gems gathered over the centuries, jewellery given by the Tsar as thanks for a service rendered or as part of a dowry. As for the stones in the Crown itself, they were the most beautiful in the world.

During the Autumn of 1990, the Soviet Union witnessed some strange phenomena. The great idol of Communism was overthrown, and people were reviving the old idols, for in the current disarray there was only the past to hold on to. One by one, the churches were opening after seventy years, and the faithful flocked in to kiss the floors and place lighted candles before the newly re-hung icons. People spoke only of the Tsar, the last one in particular. His tragic fate upset everyone, and his photograph was being sold in the streets.

Declaration of my kinship to him was to be the magic word which opened many doors. The most hermetically sealed palaces, closed by the unrelenting Soviet bureaucracy, opened as if by magic once my identity had been whispered into their custodians' ears, and thus I was able to visit otherwise impenetrable fortresses from top to bottom.

First and foremost are the great palaces which are now museums: the Winter Palace, Tsarskoye Selo, Peterhof, Pavlovsk. The last War practically destroyed them, and it has been generally accepted that the Germans, furious at not having been able to take Leningrad and forced into lifting the siege, blew them up. Except Pavlovsk, whose contents were hidden during the War, these enormous palaces are empty. So where are their great collections of paintings, tapestries, furniture, books, trinkets, silver, porcelain, miniatures and precious objects? Theft, destruction and the monstrous sales that took place after the First World War cannot entirely account for their complete disappearance. So are there still large secret depositories of these treasures?

In any event, these palaces, once destroyed, have been marvellously rebuilt since. The Communists were passionate conservationists of a past that they assassinated, and the Russians have, without question, shown themselves to be the best restorers in the world, working with infinite care, patience, meticulousness and craftsmanship. Gold leaf once again adorns the walls; lacquer panels have been replaced in the renewed wood panelling. The marquetry floors have been restored using the old designs, and the chandeliers, dripping with crystal, have been rehung from the ceilings, now repainted with frescos. The brightly-lit gilt ballrooms, their high windows shining in the night, are ready to receive their ghosts.

Other less well-known palaces, that the army or some other destructive occupants have recently returned to the Arts Ministry, are only just beginning to emerge from decades of decay, and in these only a pavilion or a few rooms have been restored recently. This is true of Oranienbaum, its exquisite follies hiding behind age-old clumps of trees. The same applies to Gatchina, where, in the English park, mills rise out of the lakes: slowly their beauty is being restored and they are coming back to life. At the other extreme is Ropcha, the palace where Peter III was assassinated by the lover of his wife, the future Catherine the Great. The experts swore that nothing remained, that the Germans had razed it to the ground. I persevered, went to the village and found the house, delapidated but still standing behind its pale blue wooden fence. There are many city and country residences belonging to the innumerable members of the Imperial family. I only had a pre-Revolution Baedeker to help me find them. Armed with a map, where the street names had for the most part been changed, I wandered round the deserted districts of the old capital and through the muddy damp woods, looking for rococo pastiches or Pompeian façades.

The majority of palaces were requisitioned by institutions. The Marble Palace became the Lenin Museum, which at the time of writing is closing down; orders have been given to throw out the mementoes relating to the Red Messiah, turned tyrant. The seat of the local Communist party used to be the palace belonging to the Grand Duke Sergei, who was assassinated by anarchists; his wife, the beautiful Aunt Ella, was thrown, still alive, down a mine shaft by the Bolsheviks. The Party has also now been expelled from this palace by order of

INTRODUCTION

IMPERIAL PALACES OF RUSSIA

the municipal council. Other buildings are occupied by trade unions, used as retirement homes, town halls or pioneer clubs, where the teachers threw us furious glances because of our disruptive presence amongst their pupils. The exteriors of these buildings were newly painted and seemed intact, resembling the photographs from before the Revolution. The interiors have been radically disfigured. But, when one looks hard, one can find here and there a ballroom freshly enamelled, incongruous in the general gloominess of its surroundings, a neo-Gothic library featuring a grand-ducal monogram, a gilded Moorish smoking room, a staircase lavishly decorated with marble *putti*. We never knew in advance what we would find, and these visits soon became treasure hunts. And we did find treasure, much of it unsuspected and unrecorded. One day, perhaps, all the palaces will be restored and open to the public.

They will always, however, be more than museums, for they were symbols in their own time, and will always remain so. In the beginning, they represented the glory of empire; then they became symbols of a detested tyranny; and, finally, they are today symbols of the eternal values of Russia, for

they are the crowning glory of the cultural heritage of a great nation and a great people.

One day, at the very beginning of the seventeenth century, Tsar Peter I appeared at the northernmost point of his Empire, 180 leagues from Moscow, on a small, flat, unhealthy, deserted island in the middle of the Neva. He struck his high boot into the muddy ground and cried out: 'This will be St Petersburg.'

Pyotr Alexeivich had not had an easy life. While still an adolescent, he had had to get rid of the Regent, his interfering and authoritarian half-sister Sophie. He had had to crush a revolt by the Pretorian guard of the Streltsy. He was still dealing with foreign wars with the Turks and with the Swedes, whose King Charles XII, an explosive genius, wanted to destroy Russia. Finally, he had had to deal with the conservatism of his subjects, who were not interested in progress. Peter had been abroad to study the development of other nations in person; he had travelled under a false name and had worked as a navvy in the Dutch shipyards. He had seen the West, and he had not forgotten the lessons he learned there.

But why build a new capital on boggy ground, in a murderous climate, next to a river which was nearly always frozen? Was it one of those caprices that the Tsars, his predecessors, specialized in? Not at all. He made his decision with relentless logic: it was the means by which he could take Russia out of its isolation and open it out to the West, to the world, to the future, and turn this inward-looking nation into a global empire. Standing in this wretched terrain, beaten by icy winds, he was able to imagine palaces, senate houses, guild halls, cathedrals, markets, entire districts inhabited by industrious foreigners.

He did not concern himself with the dangers of such an undertaking, the insurmountable difficulties, the exhorbitant cost, particularly in human life. He put at stake the destiny of his entire country, and the gamble paid off. Proudly, he laid the foundation stone of the first monument of the capital, the fortress of St Peter and St Paul. And very quickly, by 1703, he settled there to supervise the work, pursuing the architects, harassing the engineers, galvanizing the workers. He had a wooden hut built for himself, measuring 55 feet by 20. He needed only three rooms: a bedroom, a dining room and a study, all equally tiny. However, he took great care to hide the humble nature of the materials; he had the roof painted with false tiles, and the walls with false bricks. The simplicity of this residence suited the sovereign, who always hated pomp and protocol. This hut become the ancestor of all the fabulous palaces which, one by one, lined themselves along the opposite bank of the Neva.

Decorative motif which surmounts the somewhat modest entrance to the Summer Palace (see page 13). Peter I has indulged a baroque taste here: trophies and cannons refer to his military victories, and *putti* hold the Imperial crown above the Russian coat of arms.

The Summer Palace and Garden

AS St Petersburg grew, Peter the Great was obliged to live in something bigger than his hut, so he built himself a palace. The word 'palace' suggests something larger than what he actually built, for although it was better than a wooden hut, it was still very small for the seat of a great empire. His architect, Domenico Trezzini (1670–1734), an Italian from Lugano who had already built him the fortress of St Peter and St Paul, was responsible for this big, square, unpretentious house. As Peter liked the sea and boats, the house was positioned at the confluence of the little river Fontanka and the Neva. In this region of Russia, there are no stone or marble quarries, so the splendid capital was built entirely of bricks and stucco. The Summer Palace is no exception.

Both the exterior and the interior have something of that Dutch austerity that Peter the Great had so much admired during his foreign travels. He only occupied the six ground floor rooms, where he lived, worked, received guests and ate his meals. He lived very frugally, preferring to wear old clothes, worn-down boots and stockings which had been mended many times by his wife and daughters. Of course, his wardrobe contained elegant Western clothes, embellished with embroidery, lace and gold, but he never wore them. His court reflected his passion for simplicity: for him, greatness was not based on the number of chamberlains it employed – he had none, nor did he have any servants. Only two valets served him, as well as six *dentchiks*, young men who worked in shifts of two, acting as messengers, waiters, grooms and night watchmen. For his summer outings, the Tsar used a victoria carriage, which was so old that a merchant from Moscow had blushed to use it. In winter, he moved round his capital in a one-horse sledge, taking with him only one other passenger. He was in the habit of moving freely among his people, which caused a certain amount of alarm.

One day, while Peter was presiding in the 'Admiralty Armchair' over a council meeting in the modest reception hall of the Summer Palace, an unknown man appeared in the antechamber. He was carrying a small bag similar in colour to those used by the secretaries for state documents. The man waited quietly without being questioned and without attracting attention. When the Tsar appeared with his ministers, the man stood up suddenly and took something out of his bag; the *dentchiks* thought that he was a civil servant and made no attempt to stop him. At the last minute, though, one of them seized the man's arm: a quick scuffle followed and, just as the Tsar turned round, a knife

---

These two classical statues set against autumn leaves clearly evoke the romance of the Summer Garden of the Palace. The Summer Garden was opened to the public in limited numbers and many poets, including Pushkin, frequented it.

fell to the ground. Peter I grasped what was going on. 'Why did you want to assassinate me? I have not done you any harm.' 'No, but you have harmed my brothers and my religion,' was the reply. The would-be assassin was an Old Russian, an adherent of a heresy linked to tradition which Peter had pursued pitilessly in his constant effort to unify the Empire and to break the chains which held it to the past.

Peter's favourite room was his workshop, cluttered with instruments, tools, mechanical lathes and presses. Today, its most beautiful ornament is the famous machine which calculates the direction and strength of the wind, which Peter had made by Johann Dinglinger, the brilliant Saxon goldsmith. Peter I liked nothing more than to receive important guests in his workshop: men of state, ambassadors, ships' captains, architects. When calling on the Emperor, the representative of the King of Denmark, to his amazement, found him in a leather apron like any workman, leaning over a lathe working on an object in ivory. A remarkable craftsman, it was with visible regret that he left his work to talk about affairs of state with the ambassador.

He showed himself to be a tireless worker. Even in winter, when the sun does not rise until nine o'clock, he was awake by four in the morning and, still in his nightcap and wearing an old Chinese dressing gown, he would read over reports, sit in conference with his ministers and receive the senators crowding his antechamber.

After a light breakfast at six o'clock, he would go to the Admiralty to work for an hour or two, then on to the Senate. On his return to the Summer Palace, he would spend an hour in his workshop before a light lunch, followed by a siesta. At three o'clock, he would take his usual tour round the city, accompanied by his private secretary, constantly writing thoughts down in his notepad or, if he had no paper, using the first document that came to hand, scribbling notes in the margins. He would sometimes work fourteen hours at a stretch in his study; rest and relaxation were unfamiliar to him. This indefatigable man would constantly ask his entourage: 'But what do you do at home when you have nothing to do?' He himself never found the answer.

He was very proud of the kitchen that he had had installed in the Summer Palace. He hated his food to go cold, and took the initiative of placing the kitchen next to the dining room. Dishes were passed through an opening which linked the two rooms; but most remarkable of all at the time he introduced the first plumbing into Russia, bringing water from the fountains in the garden to the black marble kitchen sink. The dining-room was reserved for the family and for intimate friends; there were only eight places around the mahogany table.

His favourite dishes were cabbage soup, pork with cream sauce, cold roast meat with pickled cucumber or salted lemon. He avoided cakes, preferring fruit or cheese. He never ate fish, convinced that it did not agree with him. Meals were conducted without the slightest ceremony, and he very often ate alone with his wife, in shirtsleeves, with only a page or a lady-in-waiting present. When he invited ministers or generals, he would be served by his cook-butler, with perhaps one or two pages, who had strict orders to leave once the dessert had been served. Not without reason, Peter I was convinced that servants were all spies: 'Not only do they spy on me,' he explained to the Prussian ambassador, 'but they misunderstand everything.' When he entertained, he would sit at the table with his wife and say to the guests: 'Those of you who can find places may sit where you want. The rest of you can go home and dine with your wives.'

He hated giving receptions, and delegated this power to his favourites, particularly his great favourite, Prince Menchikov, to whom he sent tables and chairs to underline his intention. It was even at this old friend's house that he married his second wife, Catherine. Her origins are so humble that they remain a mystery. She was either a servant from the province of Livonia or perhaps even just a camp follower. A soldier passed her to a sergeant, who passed her to an officer, who passed her on to a general, who in turn passed her on to Menchikov, who offered her to the Tsar. One fine day in 1712, the latter decided to consecrate the union by marrying her. As always, it was very simple. The ceremony took place at seven o'clock in the morning, in Menchikov's little chapel, with only the required witnesses present. There followed a reception in the Summer Palace, with a little more ceremony: trumpets, drums, rich liveries and even a few coaches drawn by six horses. The groom seemed more interested in showing the guests his latest creation: a six-branch candelabra in ivory and ebony. He proudly explained that it had only taken him two weeks to make. Exceptionally, that evening, the guests were not made to drink too much Hungarian wine, a usual Court habit.

The dwarf wedding organized by the indefatigable Menchikov at his house was much more amusing to the Tsar. Peter I really enjoyed 'owning' these people whom he paid a lot for, and he was excessively proud of his collection. He liked nothing more than to hide them inside pâtés at grand dinners, to spring out when he cut the pâté open. Marriages between dwarfs were greatly encouraged, for it was hoped that they would result in quantities of little dwarfs. That day, the Tsar himself led the procession. Ministers, *boyards* and generals followed the bride and groom, who in turn were followed by seventy-two of their fellow dwarfs. The dinner was sumptuous, and the dwarfs ate at special small tables, and then the Court amused itself by watching them dance in the Russian style. That night, the best specimens of the collection were out on display: one had a huge hump on his back, another a large belly, a third rolled more than walked on two very short and bowed legs, and a fourth had an enormous head. Little piggy eyes, long ears and round cheeks were features of others in the circle surrounding the Tsar – a giant measuring over six feet six.

The first floor of the Summer Palace was reserved for the Empress Catherine, but whatever her own inclinations, she had to conform to her husband's lifestyle and the ballroom was so small that it could hold only a very few couples. Under her influence, Peter tried to introduce a bit of 'order' in his court, by which he meant decency. He cautiously began to arrange assemblies where women were present, thus limiting those solely masculine gatherings which invariably ended in monstrous drunkenness. Catherine went further and declared that no woman was ever to be found drunk, whatever the circumstances, and that men could only be drunk after nine o'clock at night.

She was the only one who dared stand up to her husband when he exploded into rages which terrified his entourage. One day, at the peak of one of these outbursts, flushed, unkempt, his eyes bulging, he broke a Venetian mirror, shouting at his wife: 'See, I can break the most beautiful object in my palace.' 'By doing so, have you made your palace more beautiful?' she replied.

IMPERIAL PALACES OF RUSSIA

The kitchen of the Summer Palace, of which Peter the Great was particularly proud. Its modernity meant that it was plumbed with running water and located next to the dining-room so that food arrived hot at the table.

Peter I's modest bedroom, with its bed no grander than that slept in by an insignificant aristocrat. The portrait of the room's illustrious occupant was added after his death.

A classical statue in the Summer Garden complemented by spring foliage.

IMPERIAL
PALACES OF
RUSSIA

18

This spirited woman succeeded her husband thanks to the machinations of Menchikov, and the former camp follower became Empress of all the Russias.

Peter I instructed his French architect Alexandre Le Blond (1679–1719) to design a summer garden next to the palace, also in the Dutch style, which he adorned with statues, fountains and pavilions. He was so proud of his creation that he opened the park to the public for festivities and celebrations, especially those commemorating his victories. The Tsar himself served the wine and beer to his veterans. The Empress Catherine and her daughters, Anne and Elizabeth, wearing the latest fashions from Paris and bedecked with jewels, graciously received their guests, including all the beauties of St Petersburg. French fashions had only recently arrived and the ambassador noted that the ladies still looked awkward in them and still believed that one of the rules of seduction was to blacken one's teeth, since only negroes and monkeys had white teeth. The guests enjoyed themselves under the bowers, and gathered round the wooden tables. The higher ranks of the clergy, in particular, took advantage of the occasion and drank unbelievable amounts of alcohol, which amazed even the most hardened drinkers.

About fifty years later, the architect and designer Yuri Velten (1730–1801) enclosed a part of the Summer Garden with the most delicate and elegant railings. Well ahead of their time, they are the epitome of neo-classical style and are one of the most delicate masterpieces in St Petersburg. Up to the end of the nineteenth century, the garden remained semi-public, open only to high society, and generations of Tsars, poets and ladies of fashion walked beneath its pleasant greenery. Countless romances were no doubt played out there, and it was the setting for many fictional scenes in Russian literature.

THE SUMMER PALACE AND GARDEN

ABOVE LEFT A view of the canal façade of the Summer Palace.

BELOW LEFT Peter the Great's study shows his preference for Dutch decorative arts, with its huge ceramic stove, heavy wooden wardrobes and elegant armchair.

Peterhof

SWEDEN was a great problem for Peter the Great. With the Swedes, and especially their King, Charles XII, war and danger were never far away. To arm himself against this, the Tsar decided to fortify the island of Kronshtadt which defended the access to St Petersburg. As usual, he wanted to keep an eye on everything, and directly supervised the building work on the fortress. In order to get there more quickly than by boat from St Petersburg, he borrowed a rowing boat from the point on the coast closest to the island.

For practical reasons, he finally had built there two wooden houses and a building to house the workers. The setting, particularly its proximity to the sea, pleased him so much that he decided to site a holiday house there. As always, modesty and simplicity prevailed, and it was more of a pavilion than a palace, built, naturally enough, in the Dutch style he preferred. He chose the French name 'Mon Plaisir' for his retreat. He had wanted it so close to the sea that you could hear the waves at all times, and during the great storms the wind and the spray prevented him from going outdoors and forced him to take his exercise in the gallery.

He entrusted the decoration of 'Mon Plaisir' to a French painter and to Nicolò Michetti (1675–1758), an architect particularly gifted at interior decoration. The bedroom and the Sea Chamber were for his personal use, whilst his secretary had an office. He made his first concession to pure decoration by creating the Lacquer Chamber, a minute room enriched with fragile chinoiserie and priceless porcelain. The Great Hall in the middle of the house served as living room and dining room, and it was here that one evening he received the ambassador of Hanover, who was very anxious to meet His Imperial Majesty. He was well rewarded, as he was ignorant of the strange customs of the founder of modern Russia.

At dinner, we were plied with so much Tokay wine, although His Majesty the Tsar himself forbode too much drinking, that by the end, we were hardly able to stand. Nevertheless, we were obliged to empty a bowl each, which was handed to us by the Tsarina herself, whereupon we became quite senseless. In this state, we were carried off to sleep, some in the gardens, others in the wood and the rest here and there on the ground. At four in the afternoon, we were woken up and returned to the pleasure house where the Tsar gave each of us a hatchet with orders to follow him. He led us into a wood of young trees where he marked out a path of about 100 paces inland from the seashore which had to be carved out of the trees. This proved to be very hard work for

---

The Marly pavilion at Peterhof, originally called 'The Little House by the Sea'.
Peter I involved himself in its location, architecture and interior decoration,
executed by Nicolò Michetti and I. F. Braunstein. The fountain was inspired by
that of Louis XIV's Marly palace, from which Peterhof's pavilion then derived
its name.

people who had not yet recovered their senses, but we followed him courageously, cutting down trees after him, and we had finished in three hours, by which time the alcohol had evaporated. One minister worked with such fury that he was hit by a falling tree and was badly bruised. The Tsar thanked us personally for our pains and forced us to follow him to supper, where we had such an overdose of liquor that we had to be carried to bed. Having scarcely slept an hour and a half, one of the Tsar's favourites was sent at about midnight to rouse us and carry us, willing or not, to the Prince of Circassia who was already in bed with his consort, where we sat by the bedside drinking wine and brandy until four in the morning. The next day, none of us could remember how we got home. We were invited to breakfast at the court at about eight o'clock, but instead of the tea or coffee we expected, we were welcomed with large cups of brandy, after which we were sent out to take the air on a high hill near the palace.

Peterhof, or 'Peter's court', as it became known, was developing. Huge forests stretched all around it, and this inveterate builder could not resist the urge to tame the wilderness. He made sketch after sketch of his ideas, which he would hand without ceremony to his planners.

The tiny and fragile Hermitage pavilion on the edge of the Baltic was designed by Alexandre Le Blond and Bartolommeo Rastrelli. It has only a single room on each floor, and its intimate atmosphere is accentuated by its surrounding moat.

The first landscape gardener was I. F. Braunstein, quickly followed by the Frenchman Alexandre Le Blond, one of André Le Nôtre's pupils, whose work here made him famous. They took the Tsar's sketches and designed an enormous park, with avenues, perspectives, rolling lawns and linking terraces. But this park needed to be furnished; the Great Palace was constructed to fit in with a complex system of pools and fountains which fed the great waterfall. Thirty thousand workers were employed on the site, for public works here were really Imperial works, as a visiting Englishwoman remarked caustically. Pavilions also appeared here and there, at the bend of an avenue, as was the fashion.

The Hermitage, that delicate construction offered up to the Baltic winds, was a refuge within a refuge for Peter the Great. To be absolutely certain of escape from courtiers and servants alike, he dug a moat around this delicate folly and installed a drawbridge. There was only one room per floor, and originally no staircase, so to get to the dining room on the first floor, a heavy machine literally lifted each guest in a special chair. The table, which could seat fourteen, was lifted up in the same way. A dumb waiter was used for the Delft plates. At the end of each course, a bell would ring to announce the next one and the guests would write their choice of dish on the menu placed in front of them.

Protected from the sea by a grassy rampart, the Marly pavilion sits at the far

OVERLEAF The front façade of Peterhof demonstrates the full grandeur of the Palace: its vastness, French inspired garden and imposing Neptune fountain.

Monplaisir was the first building at Peterhof, designed by architects Braunstein, Le Blond and Michetti. It constituted a miniature Imperial residence with its numerous bedrooms, offices, audience rooms and outbuildings.

end of an artificial lake which contained a supply of fish and on which the Tsar Peter would arrange nautical displays with gondolas and fireworks. The adjoining waterfall was inspired by that of Louis XIV's pleasure palace at Marly, which Peter had visited during his travels in France, and whose name was given to the pavilion. Peter watched over the decoration here as well, giving precise instructions to Michetti, ordering oak panelling and pine flooring. In Marly, he hung his collection of paintings which he showed to each of his visitors. As open and accessible as he was, Peter I declared that no-one could visit Peterhof without his permission, and drew up instructions as to its use. Nobody had the right to stay in the palace without a card showing the number of a bed. The visitor had to sleep in that bed and no other, and before going to bed, must take off his boots.

Peter the Great's daughter, Tsarina Elizabeth, considerably enlarged the Great Palace. Her architect, Bartolommeo Rastrelli (1700–71), added another storey onto Le Blond's structure, and added two wings. The palace was already twice as long as its original design when he lengthened it by adding two galleries each ending in a pavilion, one being a chapel topped with the usual gold onion domes, the other the so-called 'heraldic pavilion', topped with Imperial eagles. The interior decoration partly respected Peter the Great's intention, but was altered to fit the taste of the day, that of the middle of the second half of the eighteenth century, and that is how it now appears in the reconstruction made after the Second World War.

Peter I never lived in the Great Palace, and, curiously, his successors, although they all loved Peterhof, avoided it. Catherine I, his widow and successor, preferred 'Mon Plaisir', as did her daughter, Elizabeth Petrovna, and so on until the last Tsar.

Detail of the roof of Peterhof Palace. As part of his modifications of Le Blond's original palace, the Italian architect Bartolommeo Rastrelli increased the height of Peterhof, adding decorative elements such as this round window. Rastrelli worked in an Italian baroque style, but lent it characteristics particular to Russia.

This further detail of Rastrelli's roof design shows the family crest of a double-headed eagle in gold at the top of the fine onion dome.

A municipal fanfare outside Peterhof Palace. A band in Tsarist costume parades in front of the main façade to entertain the tourists queueing to visit the Palace.

27

View of Peterhof Palace, watercolour by Ivan Aivasovsky (1817–1900), 1837. The now restored Palace has hardly changed since its creation in the eighteenth century. Aivasovsky was one of the Imperial family's favourite painters, and amongst the finest Russian landscape artists of the second half of the nineteenth century.

The main fountain at Peterhof, a series of steps of gilded green marble and classical figures. In the central pool of one of the cascades, called the 'Golden Mountain', is the gilded figure of Samson wrestling a lion.

The 'Island of Olga', Peterhof, depicted in a nineteenth-century colour etching. This artificial island in the grounds of the Palace was named after Nicholas I's daughter.

The gardens and stables at Peterhof, nineteenth-century watercolour. Members of the court and visitors walking in the gardens, which were open to the public. The stables, seen in the background, were built by Nicholai Benois in the 1850s, their architecture influenced by that of Hampton Court.

IMPERIAL
PALACES OF
RUSSIA

PETERHOF

Peterhof Farmhouse, Alexander II's blue study, watercolour by E. G. Hau, 1850. The 'Farmhouse' was in fact a huge villa, now destroyed, near the Baltic in Alexander Park. Alexander II's study is typical of his taste for luxury and comfort, and is something of a triumph of neo-Gothic style.

ABOVE Peterhof Palace, the audience hall. This room is adjacent to the throne room; its double row of windows admits light to reflect off the gold and white interior.

RIGHT The magnificent staircase at Peterhof, with its marble floor and imposing gilded statues. The staircase was totally rebuilt after the Second World War, to an extremely high standard of restoration.

IMPERIAL PALACES OF RUSSIA

An overview of the Marly pavilion taken from the top of the steps of the Peterhof Palace.

Monplaisir pavilion. A view through an archway and across the exterior balustrade.

The Orangerie at Peterhof, a general view of the front façade.

PETERHOF

The Farmhouse, Peterhof, watercolour by E. G. Hau.

IMPERIAL PALACES OF RUSSIA

Right The throne room. This huge room takes up the entire width of the Palace, and is lit by windows on both sides and mirrors between. The sumptuous, over-gilded decoration reflects the power of the Russian Empire as ruled by Catherine II.

Peterhof Palace, the blue reception room. This room was reserved for the Tsar's personal secretary. Its decor has been restored as it would have been before the Revolution: the blue drapery, French furniture, Chinese and Sèvres porcelain are typical of European royal tastes.

The Winter Palace

HE history of the Winter Palace is inextricably linked with the history of St Petersburg. Peter the Great had only just begun to build his new capital when he gave orders to build the first Winter Palace, a house almost as modest as the Summer Palace. Ten years later, in 1721, the second Winter Palace was built, still modest in size and still in the Dutch style. It was here that Peter the Great died four years later at the age of fifty-two. His favourite architect, Domenico Trezzini, who had built the Summer Palace, undertook the construction of a third Winter Palace, a little more imposing than its predecessors.

As the reigns changed, so did the palace; it was altered and enlarged, swallowing up the nobles' palaces which had the misfortune to be close by. The fourth Winter Palace was occupied by the Regent, Anne, an indolent woman who ruled in place of her son, the young Ivan IV. Her parents were both German, and she surrounded herself entirely by Germans, among them her favourite ministers Osterman and Marshall München. It was a reign dominated by foreign incompetents, who were very unpopular. The true Russians, and the French, put out by the dominance of Germany, turned to Elizabeth Petrovna, the daughter of Peter the Great, Russian by descent, and Russian in spirit.

Night had fallen long before when her supporters gathered together in her house on 5 December 1741. Among them were her doctor, Lestocq, the French ambassador, La Chetardière, and her favourite, Alexis Razumovsky. The situation was perilous. The day before, the Regent had confounded Elizabeth by accusing the latter of plotting against her. The all-powerful minister Osterman had decided to send the regiments of guards loyal to Elizabeth far from the capital to the Swedish front, where the interminable war was still being fought. Elizabeth felt that all was lost. 'Of course,' said one of her supporters, 'the situation demands a great deal of courage, but where can we find it if not in the blood of Peter the Great?' Niggled by this remark, Elizabeth became herself again. She put on a breast-plate, picked up a silver cross and, at two in the morning, went through the silent and deserted streets of the snow-covered city to the Preobrzhensky barracks. She harangued the troops that had been assembled by her supporters, and they let out a loud cry in reply. 'Let's go, then, and remember that whatever happens, we must not shed blood.' She led them out.

When they were close to the Winter Palace, she got off her horse and started to walk at the head of her supporters, but the snow was too deep and the

---

The Winter Palace is probably Bartolommeo Rastrelli's masterpiece: the immensely long façade is adorned with pilasters, statues and parapets which relieve the monotony of such a vast building.

soldiers lifted her onto their shoulders. She entered the Imperial residence, despatched the sentries, sent detachments everywhere and, accompanied only by a few grenadiers, went up the grand staircase and entered the bedroom where the Regent was sleeping with her favourite, Julia Mengden. 'Wake up, sister,' she said. At the sight of the soldiers, Anne understood what was happening. She let herself be arrested, along with her offspring, the young Tsar and his sister. Elizabeth took them in her arms, 'Poor children, it is not you, but your parents who are to blame.' In half an hour, the Winter Palace had been occupied and its inhabitants rendered completely powerless. It was a quick revolution, silent and clean.

Once back at her house and in spite of the bitter cold, Elizabeth showed herself on the balcony to the cheering populace. Osterman was condemned to death at the wheel, Marshall München to having his hand cut off, followed by his head, while others were simply to be decapitated. On the 29 January 1742, the condemned were brought to the scaffold. Just at the moment when the former minister was being forced to kneel before the block and the executioner was removing his axe from its sack, a secretary of state galloped up to them, shouting 'God and Her Majesty grant you your life'. Osterman got up and with a calm voice asked one of his jailers for his wig.

Elizabeth Petrovna, who in many ways resembled her father Peter the Great, completely disassociated herself from his simplicity. Under her sister's reign, and then her cousin's, she had had to be very careful. She knew that she was

LEFT The south façade of the Winter Palace with Alexander's column, built in 1834 by Tsar Alexander I to celebrate his victory over Napoleon.

watched and feared, so she did nothing to draw attention to herself until she had seized power. Only then was she able to give free rein to her dreams. As Tsarina of all the Russias, she could at last build a palace that was worthy of her. She had already met the genius who was to leave an indelible mark on her reign. Bartolommeo Rastrelli, an Italian, had come to Russia at the age of sixteen with his father, a renowned sculptor who had received several commissions there. Bartolommeo was well versed in Western baroque, but he let himself be influenced by Russian art and architecture to the point where he created an original style, a synthesis of the two, which became known as 'Elizabethan baroque'. For thirty years, he left his mark on everything that was built in St Petersburg.

He undertook his major work in 1755. The fourth Winter Palace was demolished, as were all the surrounding buildings, and a fifth Winter Palace built, a temporary wooden structure to house the court while the sixth and last Winter Palace was constructed. An uninterrupted flow of soldiers inhabited the construction sight, where over 2000 masons from Yaroslav and Kostroma worked. The seemingly inexhaustible resources of the crown were insufficient, and Rastrelli had to appeal in person to the Senate for funds, explaining that the palace would reflect the glory not only of the Imperial family, but of Russia itself.

Rastrelli succeeded in preventing this huge construction from appearing monotonous; he alternated rows of Ionic columns with Doric ones, varied the design of the windows and peopled the flat roof with a line of bronze statues,

THE WINTER PALACE

Detail of the base of Alexander's granite column, which measures 48 metres high and weighs 700 tons.

interspersed with classical urns. The Winter Palace was finished in 1760 and the Court moved in. Two thousand people lived in it all year round and nearly twice that number were housed when the sovereign was in residence.

The ground floor was kept for administrative offices, storerooms, kitchens, servants and soldiers. The great rooms of state were on the first floor. The second floor housed the bedrooms of the countless courtiers. Elizabeth had everything in her new residence except a bedroom. She changed the room that she slept in every night, deciding at the last moment in which drawing room or boudoir she would sleep – in spite of her courage, she was always fearful of a conspiracy against her. A lover of life, she nevertheless did not mind looking through her windows to the fortress of St Peter and St Paul, the site of her future sepulchre, the Imperial necropolis; and all her successors were able to see, when emerging from the mist on the other side of the Neva, the long thin golden spire of the chapel to remind them of the vanity of worldly possessions.

In spite of the changes in fashion and the alterations, in spite of the fires, revolutions and the bombardments, two marvels survive to bear witness to Elizabeth's reign: the chapel, curiously placed almost underneath the roof, whose door carries her monogram, and the grand 'Jordanian' staircase , so named because on 6 January every year the sovereign would descend it to bless the waters of the Neva, in memory of the baptism of Christ.

Once Elizabeth was installed, she was able to realize the dream of her lover, Alexei Razumovsky. She had fished this son of a poor Cossack out of a religious choir, as his voice and looks had charmed her. They had remained faithful to each other ever after. He loved her not for her crown but for herself as a woman, and only accepted with the greatest repugnance the honours she wanted to heap on him. He was not ashamed of his humble origins and had never forgotten that his mother had had to go from door to door begging bread for her children when his drunken old father died. Thus, one day, the old Razumika could not believe her eyes when she saw a fairytale coach stop outside her hovel in the distant Ukranian village. Invited to get in, she was taken to the capital where she was greeted by a great lord dressed in silk, embroidery and lace, very different from the young barefooted shepherd who had been her son. Before introducing her to her daughter-in-law (for Elizabeth had almost certainly secretly married Razumovsky), they taught her how to prostrate herself before the Empress and made her more or less presentable by dressing her in the latest fashions from Paris and covering her in powder, jewels, and finally fitting her with a wig. Thus attired, she was hurried through a succession of rooms in the Winter Palace. Suddenly she saw before her a woman white with powder and covered with jewels. She threw herself on the ground, convinced that she was in the presence of her sovereign. It was only her reflection in a mirror; she had not recognized herself in those furbelows.

Elizabeth was beautiful, even though her figure became more than ample. She became in size what she always was in temperament – huge. She was

---

Detail of the Jordan staircase, which retains its original decoration by Rastrelli.
This painted detail shows *trompe-l'oeil* windows and classical figures. The staircase's name is derived from the practice every 6 January of the Emperor and his court descending it to attend the benediction of the waters of the Neva, in memory of the Baptism of Christ.

voluptuous and knew how to exploit it: she had herself painted naked in the guise of Venus. She was extravagant and loved clothes; at her death, they found thirty thousand dresses in her wardrobe. She was capricious: one day, about to sign an important treaty, she began to write 'Eli' when a fly landed on the paper, and it was six months before she finished the 'zabeth'. She was also sometimes violent: once, during a ball, she attacked a lady-in-waiting whose hair she found too elegant, and pulled it up with such brutality that she tore out quite a clump. In fact, she was very Russian, appealing and popular in spite of her excesses, and the last monarch to be truly of her race. Like her father, she liked nothing more than drinking sessions with men, the military mostly. These gatherings were tempestuous, noisy affairs; blue-stockings would consider them vulgar.

After the court balls, where unimaginable magnificence was displayed and where ambassadors and generals were barely permitted to kiss her graciously extended hand, she would retire to her private apartments for long drinking sessions with her favourite companions. Her court was in her image: superb, ill-managed, hiding its atavistic behaviour and Eastern excesses under the cloak of Western dress.

The years did nothing to Elizabeth's beauty, as witnessed by a young German princess who had recently arrived at her court:

> The Empress appeared before us. It is true that one cannot see her for the first time without being struck by her beauty and the majesty of her bearing. She was a large woman who, although she carried a lot of weight, was not made unsightly by it nor were her movements inhibited in any way. Her head was also beautiful. That day she wore a hooped skirt, which she only wore when she dressed up, an infrequent occurence which she only conceded to when appearing in public. Her dress was silver decorated with gold braid. She wore a black feather on the side of her head and her hair was dressed with quantities of diamonds.

The recently-widowed young woman who was discovering the ageing Elizabeth was destined to marry her nephew, the successor to the throne, Grand Duke Peter. One day she would be called Catherine the Great. She was less than enthusiastic about her future husband. She found him puerile, almost retarded, cowardly and even more hideous after his attack of smallpox.

The Pavilion Hall, situated between the Winter Palace and the old Hermitage, and designed by Andrei Stakenschneider. This is the most refined and exotic room of the palace, with its oriental fountains, crystal chandeliers, antique mosaic floors and objets d'art *carved from precious stones.*

ORANIENBAUM

INCE Peter the Great had his summer residence by the sea at Peterhof, the favourite Menchikov felt he owed it to himself to imitate the Tsar at a close location. Instead of a palace, Peter had contented himself with a modest house. Instead of a house, the upstart built a superb palace. He employed the services of the Italian architect Carlo Fontana (1634-1714), whom he had virtually monopolized and to whose services he soon added to those of the Prussian, Gottfried Schaedel (c. 1680–1752).

Oranienbaum means 'orange tree', which in wintry Russia epitomized everything that was scarce, extremely luxurious and available only to the highest aristocrats. The plan was simple: a vast central pavilion with two curved wings, each ending in two smaller domed pavilions. A gigantic princely crown rose above the central roof, witness to the vanity of its owner and his intense satisfaction at seeing his humble origins cloaked in an aristocratic mantle.

As at Peterhof, Menchikov had a canal built to the Baltic, but much bigger than his master's, and even capable of carrying warships. In contrast to the Tsar, Menchikov liked luxury. The interiors of Oranienbaum were decorated in Spanish leather, glittering with gold and silver, silk and marble. The adventurer who came from nothing had taken every precaution to insure the most opulent old age. He could not, however, insure against destiny. Peter's death and a change of monarch dragged him into disgrace. He was sent into a distant and miserable exile, having had all his property confiscated, Oranienbaum in particular.

Later, the Tsarina Elizabeth gave the palace to her nephew and successor, Peter, and to his young bride, Catherine, and Antonio Rinaldi came onto the scene. This Italian architect had already made a name for himself in his native country when, at the age of forty-three, he was invited to work in Russia. The Grand Duke Peter, in spite of his phenomenal stupidity, patronized him and, as his first task, asked him to build a small residence in the park. Peter III's palace was a very simple dwelling, modest in size and appearance, with two storeys, very much in the tradition of Peter the Great. The Grand Duke Peter exhibited another unexpected quality: he collected paintings and hung them in his residence very close together, like a patchwork. Charmed by Rinaldi's work, Peter put him in charge of the project closest to his heart: the building of a miniature fortress, of which only the entrance gate remains today. It had exercise yards, ramparts, moats, portcullises, and seemed designed for children's games. And Peter, the future Tsar, was the child. His wife Catherine wrote:

> When he arrived at Oranienbaum, the Grand Duke comandeered all his followers, the chamberlains, the gentlemen-in-waiting, Prince Repnine's adjutants, even his son, the Court servants, the hunters, the gardeners; everyone had a musket on his shoulder. He trained them every day, making them stand guard. The corridor in the house was used as a guardroom where

A corner of the Skating Pavilion at Oranienbaum, designed by Antonio Rinaldi, showing its complicated arrangement of steps and balustrading.

they spent the day. The horsemen would come upstairs for their meals and in the evening would come into the hall to dance in their gaiters. The only ladies there were me, Mrs Choglokov, Princess Repnina, my three ladies-in-waiting and my chambermaids. Consequently, the ball was very sparsely attended and very badly organized. The men were harassed and in a terrible temper from this continuous military excercise, which was certainly not to the taste of the courtiers. After the ball, they were allowed to go home to bed. In general, we were all extremely tired of the boring life that we led at Oranienbaum, where the five or six women present had to spend all their time together, isolated from others, while the men, for their part, had to exercise all day against their will.

Parading his courtiers and gardeners was not sufficient for Peter, so he spent his days exercising hundreds of lead soldiers which he had arranged on huge tables, so big that they took up an entire room. Catherine discovered him one day condemning a rat to death for having gnawed one of his toys. The body of the culprit was left hanging for three days as an example to the rest of his species.

When he was not exhausting his employees, Grand Duke Peter mistreated his violin. 'He did not know a single note,' wrote Catherine, 'but he had a good ear, and for him the beauty of the music lay in the force and violence with which he played it. The mood of the Court was not improved by having its ears battered after an exhausting day.'

Disgusted by the lack of zeal in his entourage, Grand Duke Peter had a brilliant idea: he would import soldiers from his native Holstein. He put on their uniform to receive them. The very sight of these Teutons was too much for the Russians. It was said that they were all spies in the pay of the King of Prussia, Russia's worst enemy, and the guards refused to serve them. Peter was not

Statue of a mythological figure in front of the Chinese Pavilion in the Summer Garden. There are more than eighty such statues in the garden, representing historical, allegorical and mythological figures.

Oranienbaum, nineteenth-century colour lithograph by C. Schultz, Paris. Private Collection.

IMPERIAL PALACES OF RUSSIA

Peter III's Pavilion, the first Romanov commission from the Italian architect Antonio Rinaldi. The Pavilion has six rooms on the ground floor for the servants, six on the first floor for the Tsar, where he could retreat from his wife. Built next to the Pavilion, but now demolished, was a miniature billet where Peter could indulge in his favourite pastime, exercising his soldiers.

RIGHT The seaward façade of Oranienbaum, built by Giovanni Fontana (act. 1703–1769) for Prince Menchikov, Peter the Great's favourite. Large galleries and semi-circular terraces, used as promenades, lead to the large pavilions with cupolas. In spite of its size, the Palace retains a lightness and grace.

LEFT The façade of the Chinese Pavilion, with its statue of Diana in the foreground. Catherine II had Rinaldi build this folly at Oranienbaum, where he succeeded in creating a simple masterpiece combining baroque and neo-classical elements. Its name derives only from the Chinese wallpapers used to decorate the interiors.

50

IMPERIAL
PALACES OF
RUSSIA

RIGHT The Skating Pavilion, with detail ABOVE, the most original built at Oranienbaum and perhaps of all the palace pavilions. This entertaining building, with its pyramid of stairs, columns, balustrades and vases, was designed by Antonio Rinaldi.

worried about these details: he finally knew perfect happiness, manoeuvering these human machines from morning till night. He could speak his own language with them, get drunk with them, and very soon spent all his time with them. Catherine spent the time as best she could:

> I would get up at three in the morning and dress myself in men's clothes. An old huntsman of mine would already be waiting with the guns. He had a fishing boat ready by the sea. We would cross the garden on foot, our guns on our shoulders, and get into the boat, him, me, a hunting dog and the fisherman who was taking us. I would shoot ducks among the rushes by the shore that extend for two verstes into the sea on both sides of the Oranienbaum canal. We would often forget the canal and consequently were often quite a while in open sea on this small boat.

The Grand Duchess also took advantage of her leisure to read Madame de Sevigne, and Voltaire. She was also thinking about the future and quietly preparing for it. She would often repeat to herself the predictions of the old gardener, Lamberti, who helped her design her flowerbeds. He was so old that, at the time when Elizabeth was only a princess kept very much in the background, he had predicted that one day she would be Empress; he was whispering to Catherine that one day she would be the only sovereign of Russia. He even gave the date for this event.

Much later, when she was mistress of Oranienbaum and of the Empire, Catherine added to it her most marvellous contribution. Far behind the palace, on a plateau, lay the 'upper park' where things had been deliberately left wild. Meadows were hidden amongst the trees, and torrents seemed to crash through mini-ravines. Catherine found this area charming and, showing discernment, approached Antonio Rinaldi (1709–94). She should have hated her husband's favourite architect, but she recognized his talent. He built the Empress' house for her, called 'Solitude' or 'The Chinese Palace' because of its Chinese decoration so fashionable at the time. There were quite a few problems with the wallpaper ordered from the Chinese Empire – it was late in coming and the Chinese refused to deliver until it had been paid for. It nearly came to blows, diplomatically speaking. Finally, after passing through Irkutsk, the rolls arrived at their destination. For the decor, Rinaldi surrounded himself with true artists, Stefano Torelli and the Barozzi brothers from Bologna. They trained Russian pupils and founded a school of artisans that produced the most wonderful stucco work.

For the dome in the Great Hall, Giambattista Tiepolo was asked to provide a mythological painting, which was later removed, stolen and sold abroad. The Chinese Palace is one of the most complete masterpieces in existence. The exterior is somewhat sombre, although elegant and varied. Inside, it is not particularly splendid or richly decorated, but everything is perfectly delicate and exquisite: the porcelain, the stucco, the bronze, the gilt. Nothing is overdone, as befits a place to dream in. Its inventor, Catherine, only spent forty-eight days out of the of thirty-four years of her reign in this enchanting palace.

At the same level as the big palace, at the end of a wide and long alley of old trees, stands one of the strangest creations in Russian art: the blue and white

Katalnayagorka pavilion, with its strange triangular shape, which looks vaguely like a wedding cake with too much cream. The columns, terraces, staircases and balconies all rise up in a pyramid. They came here to take refreshments, or tea, and to watch those who were playing the national sport 'Russian mountains'. There are precise and complete descriptions of this distant relation of the bobsleigh, but even after several readings its rules remain somewhat opaque.

Peter and Catherine would return to Oranienbaum every year, for as long as the Empress Catherine would allow. Even Catherine was not sorry for these visits, if only to escape the rule of their overbearing aunt. Peter continued to manoeuvre his soldiers from Holstein and Catherine was still reading her subversive authors, when in December 1761, their interfering protector, Elizabeth Petrovna, died. A few months later, the Grand Duke, now Peter III, came back to stay at Oranienbaum without his wife. He glowed with satisfaction. He had only just ascended the throne when he had ordered his troops, who were preparing to crush his inherited enemy, Prussia, to stop their advance, simply because Frederic II of Prussia was his idol. Proud of this reversal of alliances, he had just concluded a universally unpopular peace.

He was also counting on realizing his dream to divorce Catherine, whom he found too proud and too insolent, in order to marry Elizabeth Voronstova, an ugly, disagreeable, stupid and graceless woman who had the face, the manners and the mind of a servant girl, and with whom he was madly in love. From now on, he did not need to hold back. He could now threaten Catherine. He could treat her in public as an idiot. He had put up with her for seventeen years, but enough was enough, he could now exact his revenge. The Orlov brothers, Grigory and Alexei, Catherine's faithful followers, whose activities were more than suspect, were placed under surveillance. The major who had spoken of a conspiracy while drunk had been arrested. The next day he was questioned and overwhelming proof against Catherine was found, which allowed Peter to repudiate her.

That night, cuddled up to his mistress, Peter slept deeper than ever under their white satin eiderdown, in the huge canopied bed with silver and pink brocade curtains and topped with red and white feathers. The next morning, he decided to go and see what his wife was doing at Peterhof, not far away. He took his coach to his grandfather's palace and when he arrived, he was greeted by the most profound, strange and disturbing silence. There was not a sound, and no one was about: no wife, no courtiers, no servants. Dumbfounded and vaguely anxious, Peter returned to Oraniebaum. There, he found a messenger who had been able to escape from the capital, who gave him the news. He had been right to be wary of the Orlovs. The previous night, Alexei Orlov and another officer had rushed to Peterhof to beg Catherine to accompany them to St Petersburg without delay. They could only find one coach to hire, and the exhausted horses tripped and the whole enterprise was almost aborted. Alexei Orlov, never short of an idea, stopped a passing coach, unharnessed the horses, and the furious gallop continued on towards the capital, which Catherine and her accomplices reached as the sun was rising. They went to the barracks of the Izmailovsky regiment, and Catherine ordered the drums to summon the soldiers. She exhorted them to save the throne from those terrible foreigners. Surrounded by a delirious crowd, her coach slowly made its way to the palace, picking up other regiments on the way who joined the usurper. She courageously stood before the troops, wearing a Russian uniform, mounted on a white charger. A huge cry of joy, issued from thousands of throats, greeted her. The soldiers tore off the Prussian uniforms Peter III had forced them to wear, and Catherine led the way to Oranienbaum. But darkness overtook them and Catherine had to spend the night in a filthy inn, on an improvised mattress, surrounded by the campfires of her partisans.

Peter III's situation was not altogether desperate. His beloved Holstein troops received the order to resist the attack, while he took a boat to the unassailable fortress of Kronshtadt, built on a small island opposite Oranienbaum, where no one would be able to dislodge him. As he approached

ORANIENBAUM

The central façade of the Chinese Pavilion, which Catherine II had built as far away as possible from her husband's own pavilion.

the entrance to the fortress, a sentinel, at the top of a bastion, shouted down to them: 'Who goes there?' – 'The Emperor' – 'We don't have an emperor, we have the Empress Catherine.' A few shots, fired from the ramparts, soon discouraged Peter. In spite of several possible solutions, the Tsar collapsed. He ordered their return to Oranienbaum and stayed there, prostrated, and incapable of even the smallest decision.

The following morning, Grigory Orlov, Catherine's lover, approached Oranienbaum at the head of a squadron of Hussars, to inspect the palace defences. A messenger appeared carrying Peter III's surrender. Izmailov, a man completely loyal to Catherine, was delegated to take Peter III's abdication act for signature. Not only did Peter sign it, but he was forced to copy it out by hand. He asked to be left his dog, his negro, his violin and his German Bible. He was pushed into a coach with his mistress and had to pass through the middle of the crowd of soldiers shouting 'Long Live Catherine'. When he got to Peterhof, he was separated from his mistress, whom the soldiers carried off screaming. Peter threw some insults at them and their anger turned on him. They forced him to undress, and after having stayed for ten minutes with bare feet, dressed only in a shirt, exposed to their jibes, they finally threw him an old dressing gown. While the dethroned Tsar was being subjected to these appalling humiliations, in St Petersburg his wife was becoming Catherine II, soon to be known as Catherine the Great.

The gardens and the lake at Oranienbaum, with a corner of the Palace in the background.

Ropcha

HE palace of Ropcha lies about twelve miles south of Peterhof, surrounded by hills and woods. By the standards of Imperial Russia, it is small, simple and elegant, 'retiring but comfortable' according to Catherine II. The terraced gardens, surrounded by one-hundred-year old trees, lead gradually down to a big lake. It is here that, on the orders of his wife, Peter III was taken the day after he was deposed. A week passed, then, on 7 July 1762, the Empire and the entire world learned with amazement the news which the Empress Catherine II announced to her subjects:

The seventh day after our ascension to the throne of Russia, we were advised that the old Tsar Peter III was again suffering one of his attacks of haemorrhoids and was complaining of a terrible colic. Conscious of our Christian duty, we immediately gave orders to provide him with all necessary medical help. But, to our great sadness, we received the news last night that God's will had brought his life to an end.

In his reports, the British ambassador began to speak of an accident. The Saxon Minister who had seen Peter III's body exposed with great pomp, remarked that his face was as black as coal, indicating that he had suffered a violent death, as the rumours suggested. Alexei Orlov, perhaps with his brother Grigory, had gone to Ropcha. They had wanted Peter III to drink a glass into which they had poured a strong poison. Peter III, suspecting their intention, refused to drink it. A fight ensued. According to the most probable version, the assassins strangled the former Tsar. At all events, there had been violence, because very soon after a witness saw a curtain in the fateful room torn by Peter III during the fight. The brothers Orlov had wanted to dispose of the man who risked becoming a rallying point against their patron, Catherine, and who therefore remained a potential danger. The entire world accused Catherine II, and Voltaire, to everyone's indignation, attempted to excuse his friend and benefactor by saying that it was after all not that serious to send one's husband *ad patres*. In fact, when Grigory Orlov entered the widow's room to announce that 'we have done it', she fainted and then suffered terrible convulsions. Regaining consciousness, she could not stop crying: 'My glory is lost; the world will never fogive me this involuntary crime.'

This sad memory did not prevent the last Tsar's sister, the Grand Duchess Xenia Alexandrovna, from spending her wedding night in Ropcha. It must be said that, in the meantime, the palace had been considerably modified in the neo-classical style. However, her marriage was an unhappy one, and ended in a painful separation.

Until the Revolution, Ropcha was still occupied by several members of the Imperial family; today a good part of the Palace has collapsed, but the façades and the outline of the gardens are still discernable.

The Marble Palace

ATHERINE II was generous and grateful. She proved this with her favourite Orlov brother, who after all had put her on the throne and had disposed of her bothersome husband. She built the most beautiful palace in St Petersburg for Grigory, her lover. She engaged Antonio Rinaldi, who began the work in 1768. His style had evolved from the final phase of rococo which he had used so brilliantly in the Chinese Palace at Oranienbaum, to the neo-classical, with its rigour, purity and those colonnades which are the trademark of the style. The setting chosen for this palace was one of the loveliest in the city, not far from the Winter Palace, on the quay alongside the Neva. As witness to the Empress' munificence, her favourite's palace was built in marble, for marble quarries had recently been discovered in the Urals. All the other houses in St Petersburg, including those of the Imperial family, are in brick and stucco.

The noble simplicity of the exterior of the palace contrasts agreeably with the splendour of the interior. There are two elements which are more or less all that is left of the original decor: the monumental staircase, adorned with statues and frescos, and the room at the end of a wing where the decor combines the most delicate marbles, the most subtle tones and the finest bas-reliefs into a triumph of icy grace.

Catherine liked to look after her lover's every need. Not only did she not protest when he put his feet on the table, but she took great pleasure in serving him during their intimate suppers. But one day, inevitably, she began to tire of him. He felt it and it became his turn to reciprocate her generosity to him. He bought the most expensive jewel of the time, an incomparable diamond which was said to be the eye of an Indian idol torn out by a blasphemous thief. He offered it to Catherine, who accepted it. Nevertheless, she never wore it, but had it fitted into the Imperial sceptre, where it still shines, named after Orlov. For all that, Catherine did not return to her lover, who died in isolation and near-madness.

His inheritors sold the Marble Palace to the Empress. Later on, Stanislaus Poniatowski, another of Catherine's lovers whom she had made King of Poland and then deposed, lived there. In the middle of the nineteenth century, the palace was almost in ruins. It was restored and refurbished in the taste of the time by the Grand Duke Constantin Nicholaevich. After the Revolution, it became the Lenin Museum, and it was more than a little strange to see the mementoes of that great man displayed amidst completely inappropriate decor.

The Marble Hall of the Marble Palace, showing the rich variety of coloured marbles from the Urals used in the construction of the Palace. The stucco panel shows mythological figures.

Marble Palace, nineteenth-century colour lithograph drawn by J. Charlemagne.

The Marble Palace seen from the far bank of the river Neva. Catherine II had the Palace built for her lover, Grigory Orlov, by Antonio Rinaldi, whose building work extended from 1768 to 1785. Its last Imperial occupant was Grand Duke Constantine Constantinovich, the poet and playwright.

CHESME

N spite of its violent inception, Catherine II's reign was one of the grandest in the history of Russia. This little German princess governed the immense Empire with panache, authority and with that pitiless but probably necessary absolutism which disguised a great openness of mind. She corresponded with philosophers, but she still had a possible rival, the young Tsar Ivan VI, assassinated. She pushed progress forward in Russia by every possible means, but then repressed without pity the revolt by Pugachov, who claimed to be Peter III escaped from death. She won on all sides and even became a conqueror. There was a fight to the death between the Russian and Ottoman Empires. The former took advantage of the latter's decadence and nibbled away at it reign by reign. Wars were invariably followed by Russian victories. When, in 1780, the beloved Grigory's brother, Alexei Orlov, destroyed the Turkish fleet at Chesme, off the Anatolian coast, Catherine wanted to mark the event. At the time, transporting the Court involved several resting posts. They became increasingly comfortable and spacious, especially along the most frequently used routes. On the road constantly travelled between the Winter Palace and Tsarskoye Selo, she decided to build a palace at one of these relay points, in a place originally called 'The Frog Marsh' in Finnish. Catherine II changed this ungraceful name to 'Chesme'.

Yuri Velten (1730–1801) built the palace between 1774 and 1780. This architect is one of the most surprising amongst the extraordinary group of people who covered Russia with such a large number of remarkable monuments. He was Russian, with a German name, and had studied in Germany. He was director of the newly-created Academy of Art, but most importantlyof all he was responsible for containing the turbulent waters of the Neva which regularly flooded St Petersburg. Even today, his granite quays mount guard against possible disasters. Endowed with as much imagination as talent, he invented an extraordinary neo-Gothic style fifty years before it flourished in England, combined with a touch of the Orient. Chesme is his masterpiece. Its architecture is avant-garde: a triangular palace, with a tower at each corner, its geometry is perfect and it creates an impression of abstract art. Velten added a chapel next to it, in the shape of a four-leaf clover, which looks like nothing else one has ever seen. Surprisingly, unlike the palace, it is perfectly preserved, forever now surrounded by ugly and depressing workers' flats, a jewel lost in a sinister suburb.

CHESME

Details of the eighteenth-century chapel at Chesme, built by Yuri Velten in an early neo-Gothic style in the shape of a four-leaved clover. The detail LEFT shows the red and white painted stripes of stucco on the curved exterior walls.

65

TAURIDE PALACE

CATHERINE was to encounter great love with another Grigory. Potomkin was born into poverty in the Smolensk region, but this soldier of fortune quickly distinguished himself by his audacity and courage. His imposing height and bearing brought him to the attention of the Tsarina, although he lacked the fundamental qualities of classical beauty. He was more than beautiful, he was magnificent. He was the dominant male that, perhaps, Catherine II had been looking for all her life. At that time, the whole of Europe admired her and the entire Empire worshipped her. She could not resist this creature – bigger than life, blind in one eye, ugly, with a fiery temperament, indomitable courage, invincible pride and terrifying brutality. Everything had to give way or break before him. Between them, they made one of the most extraordinary couples in history; every century only has one. And even when their passion was burnt out, the friendship, the complicity, the union of two ambitions, remained: nothing could break it.

Potomkin's apartment was always near the palace, and when he arrived unannounced between military campaigns, it gave Catherine great joy. He would get up very late in the morning and dirty, unkempt, draped in a silk dressing gown stained with grease and exposing his hairy chest, his bare feet pushed into an old pair of slippers, he would appear in the Empress' chamber. Catherine, who liked order and cleanliness, never showed the slightest annoyance. On the contrary, she would go to him with a cry of joy and all the courtiers present, including the favourite and lover of the moment, would discreetly retire. Potomkin and Catherine would start one of their habitual conversations which lasted for hours. From the next room, the courtiers could hear the soldier fiercely reprimand the Empress, but none of his crude expressions ever shocked her.

Nothing illustrates the relationship between the couple better than a famous expedition which has become a legend in the Crimea. Potomkin had just conquered that region from the Turks and invited the Empress to visit it. So, with the eyes of Europe upon her, displaying her most distinguished possessions, the triumphal procession began to the sound of violins alternating with bursts of cannon-fire. The great golden boats slid slowly along the river, between the illusory villages and the ranks of peasants all aclaiming the 'Semiramis from the North', equating Catherine's wisdom and beauty with that of the famous queen of antiquity. It was the apotheosis of her reign and the height of their love. To thank him, she re-introduced the ancient mythological name of Tauride (equivalent of Iphigenia) by which the Crimea had been known and which so many Greek heroes had spoken of. She made Potomkin Prince of Tauride and gave that name to the palace she decided to build for him.

She chose a district of St Petersburg which had been recently somewhat

---

Detail of the rotunda or cupola room, showing two of the sixteen huge ionic columns and ceiling decoration.

IMPERIAL PALACES OF RUSSIA

overlooked, not far from the big convent of Smolny, where barracks alternated with waste ground. She employed a newcomer, Vasili Stasov (1769–1848), one of the first Russian architects to come on the scene and also one of the first products of the Academy of Art founded by Elizabeth. He worked on the palace from 1783 to 1789, from the start inventing a neo-classical style which could as easily be called the Russian style. This style flourished particularly in the nineteenth century and one can find innumerable examples of it all over the Empire, consisting of a simple façade, not at all severe, covered with porticoes and colonnades, with a central dome. There is no decoration; the effect is obtained through proportions and the balance between the different parts of the building. The rendering is painted that pale yellow colour so loved by the Russians. What remains of the internal decoration of the Tauride Palace, the large reception rooms, recall Potomkin's greatness, but also his soldier's simplicity. Trophies, statues of heroes and engravings are the only decorations in these vast rooms lined with huge columns.

It was in this setting that Potomkin gave an unforgettable party on New Year's Eve 1791 to thank the Empress emphatically for all her many kindnesses. The guests retained a dazzling memory of it. A first entrance hall opened out into a second of huge proportions, followed by a double row of columns leading them to the main room, which had the appearance of a huge temple. There were no furniture or ornaments, except marble vases from Carrara placed in a curve at each end of the room. Separated by a simple colonnade from the main room, the winter garden displayed plants and trees from all over the world, interspersed with antique statues. A transparent obelisk reproduced in thousands of colours the marvels of art and nature. At the end, a cave coated in ice infinitely reflected them. Through the windows, one could see the frost and ice covering the magnificent park, in the middle of which rose the statue of his benefactor, the Empress, carved in marble from Paros.

The gala was also Potomkin's farewell. He knew that he was about to die, and driven by this secret presentiment he wanted to amaze the world and to amuse himself one last time. For months, the whole city could talk of nothing but the party, and when the evening arrived the lucky ones who had been invited were quivering with impatience. It started at six o'clock in the evening with a masked ball. No sooner had the Empress arrived than three hundred musicians struck up the most brilliant symphony. She went into the main room, followed by the crowd, and took her place on a platform, surrounded by decorations and transparent inscriptions. Her grandchildren Alexander and Constantin danced in a ballet with forty-eight of the most beautiful young men and girls in society, all dressed in white and covered in precious stones. From there, the guests went into another room hung with the most opulent Gobelin tapestries, in the middle of which stood an elephant covered in emeralds and rubies, ridden by a Persian dressed in rich robes. At an agreed signal, a curtain was lifted revealing a magnificent theatre where two ballets in a new style were danced, followed by a very gay comedy. After the performances, choirs sang and dances were performed, displaying Asiatic splendour in the diversity of the costumes, each representing one of the different peoples now governed by Catherine the Great. Soon, all the apartments were opened up to the guests. The whole palace seemed on fire, the garden appeared to be covered in brilliant stones, and

The front façade of Tauride Palace. In the 1770s Catherine II decided to build a house for one of the greatest men of her reign, Potomkin. Vasili Stasov designed what was destined to remain a model for Russian neo-classicism. The Palace is simple, but not severe, with one storey, two rows of windows, a portico with six columns, two wings, and a dome to lighten the overall effect, all in perfect proportion.

Imperial Palaces of Russia

70

countless mirrors, pyramids and crystal globes reflected this magic.

A dinner was served for six hundred people, while the rest of the guests ate standing. The plates were of gold and silver and the most precious liqueurs flowed from antique cups. Officers and servants alike glinted with golden embroidery. The Empress only left the party at midnight, seemingly with regret. When she retired, several choruses struck up a hymn in her honour. She was so moved that she turned towards Potomkin to show her pleasure – he threw himself at her feet, took her hand and bathed it in his tears.

After Potomkin's death, the palace suffered many vicissitudes. Paul I, out of hatred for his mother, emptied it. Then, in the nineteenth century, it suffered several destructive retorations. Finally, at the beginning of the twentieth century, the Duma, the assembly which was the last attempt at liberalism by the Tsar, was housed there by order of Nicholas II. The marvellous winter garden was turned into a council chamber. In spite of these disfigurations, nothing could chase away the ghost of the prodigious Potomkin which still drifts through the rooms of his triumphant palace.

ABOVE LEFT The rotunda or cupola room, in fact the second vestibule of Tauride Palace. The room's columns, orchestral gallery, paintings of Hercules and enormous gilt-bronze chandelier with Imperial eagles lend this room a military air.

BELOW LEFT The Winter Garden, an enchanting eighteenth-century greenhouse where the rarest plants grew between the crystal columns and obelisks. It later became the seat of the Duma, which toppled the Tsar from power in this very room at the beginning of the Revolution in 1917.

Tsarskoye Selo

THE name of the palace in Tsarskoye Selo, 'the Tsar's village', is inextricably linked with that of Catherine the Great, although she did not commission the building of the palace. At the beginning of the eighteenth century, Catherine I, in order to make the absences of her husband bearable, chose this wooded and agreeable spot to build a holiday house, designed by one of the architects of Peterhof, I. F. Braunstein. Peter I came to stay several times, but the sea always called him and he preferred Peterhof. On Catherine's death, the house passed to her daughter, the future Tsarina Elizabeth, still an adolescent, who gave it her beloved mother's name. When she came to the throne, she was at last able to enlarge Tsarskoye Selo. She employed a myriad of talented people. Vasili Stasov, an unknown, designed a palace in the style of Bartolommeo Rastrelli. Rastrelli himself was charged with the interior decoration and with the pavilions in the park: the Hermitage, Monbijou and the Cave. A third, Savva Chevakinsky (1713–c.1767), built the church, which Elizabeth, who was very religious, wanted to incorporate into the palace and whose construction she watched over studiously to ensure that everything conformed to the strictest orthodoxy.

Tsarskoye Selo became a building site. Soldiers and labourers carried wood, bricks and iron from morning till night. One would come across worrying-looking strangers around every corner. No sooner had one building been finished than another was started. Elizabeth was cutting a little here, adding a bit more there, stretching this, finishing that, inventing left and right, until one day she realized that she would only be satisfied if she started again from the beginning. To this end, she employed only Rastrelli. Tsarskoye Selo was to be his masterpiece.

He began by raising the whole building, then, very audaciously, he lengthened the façade to make it the longest in the world: 1000 yards. No other palace could boast such an imposing presence. To avoid the monotony of such a large surface, he liberally decorated it with columns, pilastres and statues, and to show its worth, he encased it in very ornamental railings. Tsarskoye Selo became the most sumptuous palace in Europe. Its great hall, with its sparkling gilt and its long rows of windows, still gives us today an idea of the brilliance of the Court.

Sadly, Elizabeth's amber chamber was destroyed during the Second World War. Peter the Great, on his travels in Prussia, had admired some amber panels in the palace of Monbijou. King Frederick William I, sensing how much Peter coveted them and knowing what was expected of him, offered them to his visitor as a present. In exchange he received fifty-five exceptionally tall guards. The panels were placed in Tsarskoye Selo thanks to Rastrelli.

Elizabeth had never been able to do anything but follow her instinct, which

---

A detail of the gallery built by Charles Cameron for Catherine II in order for her to enjoy natural views in all weathers. A long, glassed-in room is flanked by open walkways on each side, and the elaborate, turning staircase of the gallery is decorated with bronzes.

PREVIOUS PAGES LEFT Detail of the exterior of the Turkish Bath, built in 1852 by Ippolito Monighetti (1819–1878) as a memorial to the Russian-Turkish war of 1828–29. Here a sailor rests to read outside this romantic folly.

PREVIOUS PAGES RIGHT Detail of the Marble Bridge, an exact copy of the bridge at Wilton House, Wiltshire, itself in imitation of Palladio, built in 1770 in grey marble from Siberia. The Turkish Bath can be seen in the background of the picture.

was that of excess. Catherine II, her dignified successor, was much more calculating. The inconceivable splendour of Tsarskoye Selo, and the dazzling and huge Court, were destined to display her greatness and that of the Empire. Elizabeth considered Tsarskoye Selo to be her home, whilst Catherine used it as a pedestal for her glory. She received the whole of Europe there, who on returning home marvelled at its magnificence. Her personal tastes, however, were modest and tended more towards comfort. Without touching the framework created by Elizabeth and Rastrelli, she wanted to build some apartments for herself, more in keeping with her personality. For a long time she searched for someone capable of understanding her needs. The professionals were unable to grasp what she had in mind, and presented her with models of vast residences, the opposite of what she was looking for. She brought architects from Italy, among them Giacomo Quarenghi (1744–1817), whom she employed on other projects, having, by her own admission, a mania for building: 'Building is a devilish business. It eats money and the more one builds, the more one wants to build. It's a sickness, like alcoholism, and also a kind of habit.' She wrote this very soon after finally having found the talent that would immortalize her at Tsarskoye Selo. Charles Cameron (1740–1812) was a Jacobite Scotsman, on the side of the Stuarts, a draughtsman of great talent, enamoured with antiquity, which he had closely studied. His life was to remain shrouded in mystery, unlike the almost miraculous clarity of his style.

Catherine admitted that she knew nothing about art. When Étienne-Maurice Falconet (1716–91), the creator of the famous statue of Peter the Great, asked her opinion, she answered that she did not even know how to draw. However, she was guided by her great common sense and her profound taste for simplicity. She charged Cameron with the design of an eight-roomed apartment at the extreme North of the palace, not far from the church, in the space occupied by one of Rastrelli's halls. Out of it was created the first apartment. From now on, Russia was able to compete with Western Europe, and the little German princess, who had so successfully become the incarnation of her adopted country, furnished her rooms entirely from Russia. The precious woods used for the floor were Russian; crystal and porcelain manufacturers produced the dinner services; silk factories made the fabrics that were to hang on the walls. Finally, bronze factories and the famous iron factory at Toula even provided metal furniture. The other pieces of furniture were ordered from cabinet-makers who were neither French nor German, but Russians, working in the most typical Russian wood, birch from the province of Carelia.

Cameron went on to build Catherine four other apartments, but time, and more particularly war, have damaged them terribly, though not beyond restoration. Only the first one remains, which is enough to bear witness to the genius of its creator, a supreme illustration of the grace of the eighteenth century, with poetic stylistic references to Pompeii. Catherine had had the ambition to own an 'antique house' for a long time, and in 1784 Cameron realized it for her. To the south-east of the palace is the fifth apartment, Catherine's

---

The Turkish Bath, on the edge of an artificial lake, was built in the form of a mosque with a graceful and elegant minaret – features which would never be found on a more functional bath-house.

The front courtyard and gates of Tsarskoye Selo. The courtyard was enclosed with gates of gilded wrought iron by Giuseppe Corodoni, working to designs by Bartolommeo Rastrelli. ABOVE are two details of the front façade of the Palace.

The central section of the imposing front façade of Tsarskoye Selo.

favourite, which included her bedroom. He lengthened it by adding a hanging garden which she could enter simply by opening her windows, and which led to the Cameron Gallery and to the Agate Pavilion, destined to become a Roman bath. In fact, it served as a pretext for giving a free hand, in a very limited space, to all the wealth of the Russian Empire. It had an incomparable display of jaspar, agate, porphyry, lapis lazuli, malachite and alabaster. Only the strictest elegance tempered this sumptuousness.

Catherine did not like the formality of the gardens in the French style. The eighteenth century was now drawing to a close, the fashion was changing and John Bush designed the English Park at Tsarskoye Selo, marvellously exploiting the unevenness of the terrain and its different levels to create long perspectives which opened up into meadows, and enchanted gardens of shrubs and bushes. Each of the corners of this immense and varied park have only one thing in common: poetry and romanticism. As was the mania during that period, so brilliantly inaugurated by the Tsarina Elizabeth, this park was filled with pavilions, follies and monuments which evoked every fantasy, taste, country, fashion and notable event. There was a Chinese village, a Dutch dairy, an English Gothic castle, a Greek temple, false ruins, grottoes, triumphal arches, a Palladian bridge, Turkish baths. On the great lake there were Chinese sampans, Venetian gondolas, Brazilian catamarans and a whole flotilla of miniature ships of war, along with the big gilded and decorated boats on which the Empress and her Court would relax on the water.

The Creaking Pavilion refers to a contemporary joke because its floors were made to creak deliberately. This delicious example of chinoiserie lies at the edge of a melancholy canal. Rostral columns and obelisks recall a victory over the Turks or the death of a pet hare.

One morning in spring, when the Empress was out walking, she saw a violet in the middle of a lawn; it was the first that spring, and barely open. She signalled a sentinel to approach and ordered him to keep guard over the flower to prevent

TSARSKOYE SELO

TOP The Turkish Bath with the Marble Bridge to the left. ABOVE The Chinese Pavilion, built by Ilya Neielov (1745–1793) in the 1780s. The pavilion is built of very squeaky wood, which means that it is impossible to walk around it without making a noise – an eighteenth-century joke.

The Marble Bridge, also built by Ilya Neielov. It crosses a little bay into which flow the waters of the Vittolovsky canal, filling the artificial lake.

IMPERIAL PALACES OF RUSSIA

anyone from picking it. Naturally, she forgot all about it, and more than a century later one could still see a sentinel stand guard over a violet which no longer existed, for during all that time nobody had thought to revoke the order.

Catherine the Great held Court magnificently. Knowing very well the importance of appearances, she would mount magnificent spectacles on holidays. She would enter the throne room, wearing all her medals and a small diamond crown and followed by the Imperial family. A huge cohort of courtiers would lead and follow her, with a profusion of precious stones sewn onto their clothes. These diamonds, rubies and emeralds, which glinted with each step, were calculated to dazzle strangers. It was the only Court where not only the women, but also the men covered themselves with jewels. In this way did Catherine greet a deputation of Poles. They refused to let themselves be impressed and kept up a mocking and hostile look. The Empress lifted them out of their prostration with solicitude but also with an air of grandeur. Each one in turn was presented to her, and advanced to go down on one knee. She talked to them. She had a sparkle, a radiant look, which made an impression on everybody. She only kept them a quarter of an hour. When she retired, she curtsied to them so graciously that they involuntarily returned it with a deep bow. They all left saying: 'No, she is not a woman, she's a siren, a magician, one cannot resist her.'

In spite of this pomp, Catherine really preferred intimate evenings among friends. Russians outnumbered everyone else in her circle, but a few distinguished strangers mixed in with them. She published a famous set of rules amongst her friends which, in this period of strict etiquette, could be construed as a true manifesto of social revolution. This sovereign, who had made absolutism triumph, was looking for equality, liberty and even a sort of fraternity with those whom she admired. They would chat and act out plays which Catherine herself had written. These were not perhaps very good literature, but her friends enjoyed rehearsing them. At the Winter Palace, she asked Velten to build the first Hermitage for these reunions and to house her growing collection of pictures. She also had a small theatre built next door by Quarenghi. But while in the capital, she had little leisure to dedicate to her friends, and she was better able to spend time with them at Tsarskoye Selo. She would wait impatiently every spring for the time to leave, and she travelled there in a large coach pulled by ten horses, preceded by six valets, twelve hussars and twelve Cossacks from the Guard, and followed by pages and equerries, all on horseback. No sooner had her carriage set off than one hundred cannons fired to announce her departure. The populace would then rush to try and catch a glimpse of their beloved sovereign.

Countess Golovin was a faithful witness to the exquisite life led at Tsarskoye Selo. Her youth made the close circle which surrounded the Empress appear a bit decrepit, and around her she could only see old field marshals and equally ancient ladies-in-waiting. She began by being the playmate of the Empress' grandchildren, Constantin and the eldest, Alexander, his grandmother's favourite. One day, while dancing the polonaise with the little Golovin, he announced that he would show her a 'horror'. Embarrassed but intrigued, the little girl folllowed him right to the end of the apartments. In the last room Alexander pointed to an antique statue of Apollo standing, completely naked, in

The White Pavilion, a tiny, one-room structure in the gardens of the palace close to the Concert Hall. This details shows a caryatid, one of two on either side of the entrance to the Pavilion.

IMPERIAL PALACES OF RUSSIA

a corner. And the 'horror' in question was the part of his anatomy which should have been covered by a fig leaf.

In spite of the rumours that mother and son were not getting on, it was the time when, according to Countess Golovin, the Empress and her successor, the Grand Duke Paul, would see each other every morning and evening, and when their relations were very harmonious. Catherine II was so considerate that she would have a blind lowered if the sun was disturbing someone. She was playing cards one day, and one of her usual companions, Chertkov, a bad player, grew impatient because he was losing and threw his cards in her face. She did nothing, but stopped the game. Chertkov took control of himself and felt crushed: never again, of course, would he have access to his idol's intimate circle. The following day, he stayed in his corner, feeling his world had come to an end. Catherine noticed him, took him by the arm and made him take a turn round the room: 'Aren't you ashamed of having imagined that I would hold anything against you? Have you then forgotten that between friends quarrels can never last?' 'Oh, mother,' he replied, using the familiar form of address, 'how can I speak to you, how can I respond to such goodness? I would always want to die for you.' Countess Golovin added: 'The familiar form of address is very energetic in Russian and does not detract from the respectful language.'

In the mornings, the young Golovin would see the Empress on her terrace, sitting at her work-table on a green leather sofa. She would read and write from dawn onwards, next to flowerbeds filled with fragrant flowers. In the evenings, the Empress would call for crayons, pens and paper. People would draw, play parlour games and conversation would flow freely. They would take walks; the weather was so beautiful and balmy that they would return to the palace with regret. Catherine would stop under the colonnade to admire the setting sun, to breathe in the scent of the flowers and to be caressed by the soft air. She would allow her grandchildren to take excursions in the surrouding countryside. The Grand Duke Alexander had in the meantime married the ravishing Elizabeth of Baden. They took the little Countess to Tsarskoye Selo to pick flowers in the fields and to look for rare herbs for the herbalist's album. Or they would go the one of the villages recently settled by Germans, who would play waltzes from the Rhine valley, cook an omelet and serve them butter and cream.

They also played sport, and games were played on the lawn, where they were divided into two sides, Grand Duke Alexander's with a pink flag, and Grand Duke Constantin's with a blue one, embroidered in silver with their monograms. Countess Golovin was, of course, always in Alexander's camp. The Empress would watch the game sitting on a bench on the edge of the lawn. She would gaze at her favourite, the last one to hold that title, the egregious Platon Zubov. He in turn would be gazing at the wife of the Grand Duke Alexander, Elizabeth, with whom he was in love. Countess Golovin never forgot this happy time:

> This period was quite stormy, but it was also one of great joy. It seemed to lend itself to those illusions which so seduce the young. That imposing Court, that palace, those gardens, those terraces perfumed with flowers, gave one chivalrous ideas and inflamed the imagination. At the end of one walk, on the most beatiful evening, the Empress stopped on the ramp. We sat down on the

Musicians playing Mozart beside the High Bath pool in front of the lake façade of Tsarskoye Selo.

84

large paving stones which bordered it. Her Majesty placed me in between her and the Grand Duchess, whom Zubov could not keep his eyes off. Suddenly, we heard divine music. Dietz, a distinguished musician, was playing a trio on his *viola d'amore*. He was accompanied by an alto viol and a violin-cello. This orchestra was playing by Zubov's window , not far from the ramp. The harmonious sounds of this instrument of love lingered in the air, the surrounding calm prolonging its effect. The Grand Duchess was moved.

Detail of the exterior of the Concert Hall at Tsarskoye Selo, built by Giacomo Quarenghi in a pure, neo-classical style for Catherine II.

Her youth and innocence prevented the Countess Golovin from seeing, or wanting to see, that Catherine the Great, between her roses and her dogs, also cultivated an extraordinary succession of lovers, each one more beautiful than the last. Whilst acting in this capacity, their existence was kept within strict limits. Their apartments were designated in advance, along with their pensions, the honours they would receive, almost even the length of their favours, followed by their golden retirement when another had replaced them.

Meanwhile, Catherine II was growing old. She suffered from gout and rheumatism. It became more and more painful for her to go down, and especially up, the staircase that Cameron had built her at the end of her Gallery. The Scotsman then offered her his last contribution to Tsarskoye Selo, that *pente douce* as it was called in French, which allowed her to reach the garden from her first floor apartment without effort. At sixty-seven, she remained beautiful and almost desirable. She always presented herself with taste and simplicity, impeccably dressed and with her hair carefully arranged. She was not small, but had grown considerably fatter with age. Even though she was corpulent, she remained infinitely graceful.

The visit from the King of Sweden had disappointed her; he had refused to marry her granddaughter. It had also tired her with an uninterrupted series of galas. Her legs swelled up, and wounds opened that would not heal. She had been so proud of her tiny feet but no longer showed them. However, on this 4 November 1796, she felt happy. In reality, there was nothing she hated more than the French Revolution, whose impact she was measuring and whose implacable enemy she had always been. She had just received news of the counter-revolutionary armies. Her large equerry who often served as her jester, Leon Natichkin, made her laugh so much that it gave her a slight colic and she retired a little earlier than usual. The next day, she got up at her usual hour, and called for her favourite, Platon Zubov, who came by the internal staircase. She kept him for only a few moments, and sent him back into the antechamber to wait for her. Time passed. Her valet, Zachary Constantinovich, was surprised that she had not called him. Hearing no sound from the room, he finally took his courage in both hands and opened the door. He found Catherine II on the floor, unconcious, lying in front of her commode, in between the two doors which led from her bed-recess to the night-commode.

They called the doctors. There was chaos and consternation everywhere. Was the Empress dead? No, she was still alive, for her heart was still beating, but there was no other sign of life. The successor to the throne, Grand Duke Paul, was in his own palace at Gatchina, to which messengers were sent. Six or seven of them arrived at the same time, but could not find him, as he had gone several miles from there to see a mill under construction. They found him at last. Having been told of the situation, he rushed with his wife to the palace, and arrived at eight in the evening, where he found total confusion. He could however lay his hands on only a few ministers and courtiers, for the others had disappeared, nobody knew where. Paul and the Imperial family surrounded the unconscious Empress. She was lying, completely still, on a mattress thrown on the floor near where she had been found. Her successor, who had never loved his mother and by whom he had always been badly treated, did not lose his head. He gave instructions as if he was preparing a theatrical spectacle. His own courtiers arrived from Gatchina, unable to hide their impatience. As for those belonging to Catherine, one could read the despair on their faces. Countless coaches and other carriages of all kinds jammed the approaches to the palace, waiting for the unthinkable event. Towards ten o'clock in the evening, Catherine seemed to revive, only to begin a death-rattle so horrible that the young Grand Duchesses had to be removed from the room. Finally, she let out a terrible scream, so loud that it was heard in all the surrounding apartments, and finally died after thirty-seven dreadful hours.

Pavlovsk

ATHERINE II had never got on well with her only son Paul. In spite of this, when he produced a son Alexander in 1777, and she knew that the future of the dynasty was at last assured, she made him a generous gesture. She gave him and his wife, Maria Feodorovna, a property of 1500 acres to the south of Tsarskoye Selo. At the time, it was a region covered in dense forests through which flowed a tiny river, the Slavyanka. The property boasted only two wooden hunting lodges called 'Crick' and 'Crack'. The new owners decided to start modestly by building two wooden houses, which they named 'Paul's Joy' and 'Maria's Valley'. Catherine, who had recently become infatuated with the architecture of Charles Cameron, suggested that they use him or, rather, forced him on them, for in fact as the one holding the purse strings she decided everything. She had always been generous with her lovers, but she was very mean with her children, to the point where they had to write humiliating letters asking for an increase in their funds.

Paul and Maria liked Pavlovsk so much that 'Paul's Joy' and 'Maria's Valley' soon seemed too small for them. They decided to have something bigger and more solid. In spite of the fact that neither of them really liked Cameron's style, they did not dare approach anyone else to build them a palace in 1781. Maria Feodorovna thought of everything. The first thing she had built was a temple of friendship for her formidable mother-in-law. While one cannot doubt the suitability of such a gesture, one can doubt its sincerity. Cameron presented the plans for the new Pavlovsk to the Grand Duke and his wife, who no sooner had they approved it, left for a long tour of Western Europe, leaving the task of overseeing the work to the Empress. They could not have given her more pleasure than by encouraging her passion for building.

Cameron had been imposed on Paul and Maria, and he would pay dearly for it. From abroad, they bombarded their administrators with letters (they did not dare write to the architect himself) asking them to make Cameron execute modifications. He became exasperated. He wanted to control everything himself, decide everything right down to the last detail of decoration. To Cameron's fury, Paul and Maria went on a shopping spree abroad, buying tapestries, furniture, porcelain, silver and chandeliers without knowing where they might put them. During this journey, Maria Feodorovna became firm friends with Marie Antoinette, whom she always greatly admired, and she and her husband were sumptuously received at the French Court. When they visited the Sèvres factory she went into ecstasies over a magnificent dinner service of several hundred pieces which was just being finished. She was asked to lean over and look at the monogram displayed eveywhere on it: she recognized her own, for this was a present that the Queen of France was giving to her new friend.

Monument to the parents of Paul I's wife, Maria Feodorovna. This detail, showing the profiles of mother and father, is part of a small pavilion in the gardens of Pavlovsk.

As for Cameron, he was still torn between Catherine on the one hand and Maria Feodorovna on the other, between Tsarskoye Selo, where he was needed and Pavlovsk, which was behind schedule. He was being driven slowly mad. On her return to Russia, Maria Feodorovna soon had reason to be worried. In an unexpected act of generosity, Catherine II had just given her son another palace, Gatchina. Even though this one had been built for and given to Grigory Orlov, who he regarded as his father's murderer and therefore hated, he accepted the gift and loved living there. Gatchina was in effect the epitome of the military style that pleased him so much. Maria Feodorovna began to create a fuss. She did not want Gatchina, she liked her Pavlovsk and did not intend to move at any price. She insisted so much that her husband gave it to her outright. Mistress of her own house at last, Maria Feodorovna decided to make her own contribution to Pavlovsk. She tried to employ another architect, Quarenghi, but the latter, a loyal man, refused to play the game. So she approached Cameron's assistant, Vincenzo Brenna (1745–1820); this opportunist did not stand on his honour. He was prepared to work for the Grand Duchess, thus taking his master's place.

Cameron had wanted a Palladian look. Brenna added one floor on the southern gallery and two pavilions, linked by curved wings, two storeys high, which almost formed a closed courtyard, thus radically altering the original plan. He succeeded in surrounding himself with the best decorative painters and sculptors of the time, Andrei Voronikhin, Quarenghi himself for the design of two rooms, and Carlo Rossi, who began his career here.

It was the period of the first great archaeological digs, of the antique revival and of the Grand Tour, so Pavlovsk boasts an Egyptian entrance hall, a Greek room and an Italian room. Paul I was fascinated by the idea of war, and to evoke the conflicts in which he never took part there was a War salon and a Peace salon. There was also a Knights' room; after Bonaparte had seized Malta, a few knights had escaped to Russia, and Paul I, with a long term political objective in mind, had, quite illegally, appointed himself Grand Master of the Order.

Marvellously reconstructed after its destruction during the Second World War, the decor in Pavlovsk is more enchanting than that of any other. Everything in it is exquisite and every detail shows refinement. The door handles are signed Goutière, and ivory and ebony have been incorporated into the parquet floors. But most of all, Pavlovsk is built on a human scale. One could easily live there, whereas the idea of living in the immense palace of Tsarskoye Selo fills one with dread. Complete harmony reigns at Pavlovsk thanks to the most expensive simplicity, but the palace does not throw its wealth at its visitors. It is supremely delicate and seems a very moving spectacle in the implacable climate of these northern steppes. Pavlovsk has the appearance of something fragile and indestructible at the same time. It is not an imposing palace, it is the house of a gentleman and a honest man, even if he happens to be the richest and most powerful on earth.

ABOVE RIGHT The Gardens of Pavlovsk, nineteenth-century watercolour. The gardens were laid out by Charles Cameron, Vincenzo Brenna and Pietro di Gottardo Gonzago and divided into seven sections, alternating open expanses with enclosed spaces, water, classical pavilions, bridges, and sculptures. **BELOW RIGHT** A general view of the Palace across the gardens.

PAVLOVSK

IMPERIAL
PALACES OF
RUSSIA

Classical statues in the Gardens of Pavlovsk, with NEAR RIGHT the colonnade of Apollo at the head of a waterfall and RIGHT a portico with Ionic columns designed by Charles Cameron, encircling a copy by Paolo Triscorni (1797–1832) of the three graces by Antonio Canova.

FAR LEFT One of the most elegant bridges in the gardens, decorated with statues of centaurs. LEFT The Temple of Friendship, designed by Charles Cameron and dedicated to Catherine II by her daughter-in-law. It is surrounded by fluted Doric columns, the first to be used in Russia. BELOW The front courtyard of Pavlovsk in stormy weather.

IMPERIAL
PALACES OF
RUSSIA

RIGHT Paul I's study, situated amongst the common family apartments in the Palace. FAR RIGHT The lantern drawing room, Maria Feodorovna's study, considered to be the masterpiece of architect Andrei Voronikhin (1759–1814). Caryatids by the sculptor Vasili Demuth-Malinovsky (1779–1846) support the arch which separates a protruding bay from the rest of the room. The walls are hung with Italian and Spanish paintings by Carlo Dolci, Guido Reni and José de Ribera.

IMPERIAL PALACES OF RUSSIA

ABOVE A view from the Hall of Peace through to the Greek Hall and the Hall of War. The Hall of Peace uses cornucopia, garlands, flowers, musical instruments and rural symbols as its decorative devices.

RIGHT A boudoir, which Maria Feodorovna described thus: 'The fireplace has a pediment supported by two columns in porphyry and jaspar, with a big marble vase in the centre. From the balcony I have views over the small garden and a large part of the park.'

OVERLEAF The Greek Hall, with its fluted columns, pilastres painted in imitation of ancient green marble, white marble vases and Corinthian capitals. The marble chimneypieces are encrusted with lapis lazuli and bronze, and the room is lit by two bronze lanterns.

IMPERIAL PALACES OF RUSSIA

PREVIOUS PAGES LEFT One of three charming rooms which served as antechambers for those waiting to be received by Paul I. This links the picture gallery to the throne room. PREVIOUS PAGES RIGHT Maria Feodorovna's state bedroom, lavishly decorated with malachite, jaspar, agate, lapis lazuli and gilt bronze.

The park is the most picturesque of all the Imperial residences, full of winding paths, charming surprises and unexpected discoveries. It is generally attributed to Cameron himself, but a seductive, if not well-supported, theory suggests that it was Capability Brown who furnished the plan, through one of his old pupils, Gould, who had been Potomkin's gardener. Maria Feodorovna was particularly attached to a pavilion called 'Apollo's colonnade' which a terrible storm half knocked over one night. They wanted to restore it, but the Empress had the prescience to leave it as it was, thus inventing the first true fake ruin. In her beloved domain, she led a life which suited her. She played music, painted, made engravings, embroidered, created objects in ivory and left numerous examples of her talents. She read and wrote, but most of all dedicated herself to her charities. She built schools, hospitals and maternity clinics. She organized the vaccination of children and she founded the first school in Russia for the deaf and dumb, which was a great success.

Maria Feodorovna was absorbed in her own personal pleasures and entertained badly. First of all, unlike the past, future and contemporary members of the Imperial family, she was careful with money. Life at Pavlovsk, according to a visitor, was a deadly bore. Visitors would take measured walks in the park, one behind the other, and meet again for interminable gatherings. The Emperor, Empress, Grand Dukes and Grand Duchesses would sit in armchairs in a circle, while others sat on stools. Only a few banalities were exchanged; conversation languished. Nobody had the right to stand up and leave, by order of the Emperor! As in everything else, he was the opposite of his mother, and

ABOVE LEFT The centaur bridge and Apollo pavilion, nineteenth-century watercolour. ABOVE RIGHT Nineteenth-century watercolour depicting Pavlovsk from its gardens, a scene which has changed very little since. RIGHT A detail of Maria Feodorovna's library, its austerity relieved by the elaborate armchair designed for her by Voronikhin, and by biscuitware figures.

OVERLEAF The Picture Gallery was designed to house the collection of paintings by Gerard Terborch, Gabriel Metsu, Paolo Veronese and Peter Paul Rubens that Paul I and Maria Feodorovna acquired during their travels in Europe while still heirs to the throne. The Gallery is nevertheless decorated and furnished in elaborate Russian style.

IMPERIAL
PALACES OF
RUSSIA

TOP The Italian Hall, a rotunda situated next to the Greek Hall and inside the central cupola of the Palace. A detail showing *trompe-l'oeil* marble and classical figure.

ABOVE Monument in the gardens of Pavlovsk enclosing a forbidding statue of Maria Feodorovna.

RIGHT When Napoleon Bonaparte seized Malta, the remaining Knights of that Order fled to Russia. Paul I had this Knights' Gallery built to receive them. The architecture is simple, with pale green walls, white stucco friezes and several Roman sculptures, some authentic.

IMPERIAL
PALACES OF
RUSSIA

The Italian Hall is situated at the centre of the Palace, extending the entire height of the building. It is lit by a chandelier hung from the lantern which surmounts the central pavilion of the Palace.

The Drawing Room of the common family apartments. This room is refined to the point of austerity by Russian standards, with walls painted to imitate blue marble and luxurious blue and yellow curtains.

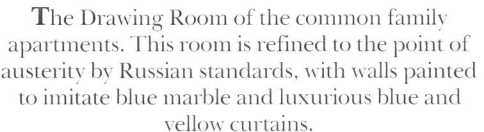

PAVLOVSK

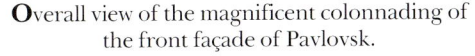

Overall view of the magnificent colonnading of the front façade of Pavlovsk.

A view of the gardens, with a gentle and endearing lion sculpture.

IMPERIAL PALACES OF RUSSIA

people would sigh with regret when they remembered the delightful evenings spent with Catherine the Great. In fact, Maria Feodorovna, as a true German, and in advance of social fashion, was a good middle-class woman. In contrast to other Empresses, she liked only to be with her family, behaving like a mother hen towards her children and profoundly attached to her husband. She credited him with every quality, every virtue, and she was probably the only one in the Empire to do so.

Paul I's appearance was Mongolian, with his splayed nostrils, high cheekbones and drooping eyes. A witness, who clearly did not particularly like him, described him thus:

> He has not improved since he has grown older, bald and wrinkled. The Empress, when she appears with him, seems like one of those ladies who have a horrid little monkey or negro painted next to them to enhance their height and beauty. His odd clothes and the awkwardness of his manner emphasize his ugliness. Including even the Kalmyks and the Kirghises, Paul is the ugliest man in his Empire, and he even finds himself so ugly that he will not have his face stamped on the coins.

All his life he was tortured by the idea of being illegitimate, a possiblity which has been hinted at since, but so many of his traits remind one of Peter III.

A view of the Monument to the parents of Paul I's wife.

This gracious little pavilion designed by Charles Cameron was used as an aviary, an indispensible feature of all eighteenth-century Russian country houses.

At Pavlovsk, he had a vast excercise yard installed where he would amuse himself by exercising two artillery regiments garrisoned close by simply for that purpose. His other distraction consisted in placing as many sentinels as he could on a particular covered terrace. Then, hiding behind a shutter, he would spend a great part of each day armed with a telescope observing them in order to control their posture and to reprimand them at the slightest movement.

One day he confined all the officers of a batallion to barracks for having saluted incorrectly. Another day he spat on an officer who had fallen off his horse and, because his leg was broken, had not been able to stand to attention. He did not hesitate to hit captains and majors for the slightest error. He sent an officer, who had the misfortune to pick up his arms too soon after he had passed by, to Siberia. He took delight in resurrecting the most obsolete and humiliating customs in Russian history. For instance, no sooner had one seen his carriage than one had to get out of one's own carriage and prostrate oneself with one's forehead on the ground, even in the mud or the snow. Heaven help anyone who did not bow down soon enough or low enough: people were sent to Siberia on a whim. Basically, with soldiers as with civilians, Paul became more and more niggling, tyrannical and unbearable. Fundamentally, he was not a bad man, but a modern psychoanalyst would say that he was uncomfortable in his own skin. He had been insufficiently loved and was a solitary man, full of complexes.

View of the gardens, looking towards the Friendship Pavilion and showing the artificial river landscaped into the gardens.

Old Michael's Castle

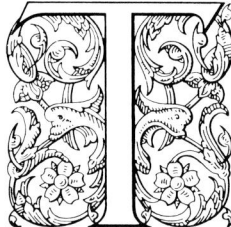

TSAR Paul was still looking for a house exactly to his taste. Pavlovsk now belonged to his wife Maria Feodorovna, and Gatchina was too far away. The supernatural now came to his aid, when a guard at the Summer Palace had a vision one night. St Michael suddenly appeared before him and spoke some incomprehensible words, which Paul translated as meaning that he wanted a church dedicated to the Archangel built on this spot. Without hesitating for an instant, Paul had the wonderful wooden palace built by Bartolommeo Rastrelli for the Tsarina Elizabeth Petrovna razed to the ground. He had been born in that Summer Palace, and perhaps this destruction was not without deep psychological significance. Wanting to replace it with a palace which conformed exactly to his wishes, he gave the most precise instructions to the architect he had chosen. Vasili Bazenov (1717–99) was a slightly tragic and mysterious figure, which must have pleased the Emperor. He was already old and sick, and had studied in Paris and Italy. He presented several very appealing schemes and each time the project failed, as if bad luck was following the poor man. Paul obviously owed it to himself to employ an architect that his mother, Catherine II, had treated badly. But Bazenov's state of health prevented him from keeping an eye on everything, and Vincenzo Brenna, the architect of Pavlovsk, came to the rescue.

The new palace still seems extraordinary today. From a distance, the red cube looks like a fortress, which is as Paul had intended. The octagonal courtyard is an architectural *tour de force*. Naturally, the façade incorporates a large church dedicated to St Michael, as promised, and Maria Feodorovna gave birth to a son at the palace whom Paul named Michael. Old Michael's Castle has a unique and wonderful position, placed as it is between the Summer Garden, the parade ground and the canals. However, for reasons of security, Paul had insisted that it be built on an island, and it is consequently particularly damp. This castle had something sinister about it from the beginning. The mistrustful Paul had a trap door made which went from his room into an underground passage leading to the barracks of the Pavlovsky regiment, on the other side of the parade ground. He was then able to find refuge amongst his dear soldiers should the need arise.

He was more and more impatient that the Castle be finished, as if he could sense from somewhere that he had little time left. On his orders, materials were taken from wherever they could be found, so, for instance, a frieze destined for the new cathedral of St Isaac was incorporated into a wall. Paul literally pillaged the palaces built by his mother for her lovers in order to furnish his residence with the greatest possible haste. In particular, he completely emptied the

Old Michael's Castle, nineteenth-century colour lithograph drawn by J. Charlemagne, Paris. The front façade of the Castle, with a statue of Paul I. His decision to build the Castle on the site of the wooden summer palace where he was born was inspired by an apparition of St Michael to one of his soldiers. The Castle bears the name of the archangel.

Tauride Palace, Potomkin's former residence. Finally, he wanted his monogram everywhere, and a particularly patient researcher who wanted to count them stopped at eight thousand.

The first stone of Old Michael's Castle had been laid in November 1797, and at the beginning of 1801 Paul I already insisted on living there. On 1 February he moved in with the Empress and his two sons, Alexander and Constantin. As the sons' apartments were not yet ready they had to live in an antechamber and their wives stayed behind at the Winter Palace. A few weeks later, together with their children, they rejoined their husbands. The carnival was nearly over. Paul I, in his joy at having finally moved in, gave an inaugural ball in his new home. Then, once the fireworks were over and the violins had stopped playing, he settled into his sombre routine. His mistrust cut him off more and more from the world, starting with his wife and children, who were nonetheless very loyal. He saw enemies and traitors everywhere. He suspected plots against him. His cruel manias became more and more obsessional. But Paul I was far from being stupid. He had a quick intelligence, a lively mind and was a very clear thinker. He even showed extraordinary prescience in foreign affairs. He forecast the domination of the young Bonaparte whom the whole of Europe said would not last, although he hated France and its revolution and was a staunch ally of England. Suddenly, for reasons largely unknown, he made a spectacular change of alliance, abandoning England and making a *rapprochement* with France.

A few weeks passed. On 11 March 1801, Paul left the castle in the evening, and as was usual, spent the evening with his friend, Princess Gagarin. Finding him paler and more sombre than usual, she asked him anxiously what was the matter. 'The matter is that it is now time for me to make my move, and in a few

Imperial Palaces of Russia

days they will see the heads of my loved ones roll.' The Princess shuddered. Paul had already made threats against his wife. He had even had his eldest son arrested. How far were his suspicions going to take him? On the first pretext, the Princess leapt out of the room, scribbled a note addressed to the heir to the throne and had it taken to Old Michael's Castle.

The Tsar returned to the castle at eleven o'clock. He went into his apartments, got into bed and fell asleep straight away. At just the same time, a group of conspirators were leaving the Talitsin Palace where they had spent the evening. There were about sixty of them, lords and officers who had been mistreated or disgraced by Paul, or who could no longer put up with his tyranny and dreamt of liberty. They had planned their coup for weeks. Wrapped in their coats, and making sure that they were not recognized, they walked silently towards the castle. Among them were Platon Zubov, Catherine's last favourite, Count Pahlen, governor of St Petersburg and leader of the plot, Count Beningsen and many more. They entered by the garden door. As they were passing under the great bare trees, their steps woke a whole family of crows who flew away cawing lugubriously. They saw this as a terrible omen. When they reached the castle courtyard, they separated into two groups. Pahlen led the first one. He slid into the castle through a particular door that he knew well, as his function put him in daily contact with the Tsar. He had also taken care to replace the usual guards of the place with soldiers who supported their cause. He had, however, forgotten one post. 'Who goes there?' he heard. He approached and opened his coat to reveal his jacket covered with decorations. 'Can't you see where we are going?' 'Your patrol may pass,' replied the sentinel.

They reached the gallery which preceded the Emperor's antechamber, where they found a co-conspirator, an officer dressed as a soldier. 'Where is the Emperor?' asked Zubov. 'He has been back an hour and is no doubt now in bed.' The officer knocked on the door. 'Who's there?' He recognized the voice of the Emperor's valet. 'Me, Aparkamakov, His Majesty's aide-de-camp.' 'What do you want?' 'I've come to make my report.' 'You must be joking. It's midnight.' The aide-de-camp insisted, the valet hesitated, and finally opened the door. The conspirators immediately threw themselves into the antechamber. The valet was too frightened to react, but a Polish hussar threw himself in front of the door, yelling 'Sire, you must escape.' He ordered the conspirators to move back. A pistol shot rang out. The brave hussar soon found himself disarmed and pinned down on the floor. The shot, rather than the cries of the hussar, had woken Paul with a start. He jumped out of bed and ran towards the hidden door which led into the Empress' apartment. He tried without success to open it, forgetting that, in his mistrust, he had recently had it blocked up. He then remembered the trapdoor leading to the underground passage, but his bare foot was not strong enough to work the spring. His way to salvation had been blocked.

He heard the conspirators trying to break down the door, which finally gave way under the pressure. Beningsen and Zubov ran to the bed, which was empty. 'All is lost, he has escaped.' 'No,' cried Beningsen, pulling the screen placed next to the bed. Behind it cowered the Emperor of all the Russias. He called Pahlen to his aid, whom he considered to be his most faithful supporter. He did not understand what was going on, nor what these men wanted. Beningsen and Zubov tried to explain that they came in the name of the Senate to obtain his

Paul I wanted the Castle to act as a fortress, yet its architects, Vasili Bazenov and later Vincenzo Brenna, succeeded in making it livable. The rich colour of the Castle's rendering, the bas-reliefs of the façade and the chapel on its western side lend it a certain beauty.

abdication and handed him the Act to sign. Paul approached the lamp placed on the mantelpiece to read the document. As he read it, his violent temper returned. He began to protest. They replied with insults. He again began to read. Anger overtook him. He forgot that he was alone, unarmed and almost naked, among these armed and purposeful men. He crumpled the Act of Abdication with a furious gesture and threw it on the floor. 'Never. I would rather die.'. Did he make a move to reach for his sword, placed next to a chair, as the conspirators claim? We shall never know.

At this point, the second group of consipirators, who had taken a different route, erupted into the room, among them Prince Tatetsvil, bent on revenge after having been insulted by Paul. He threw himself at the Tsar, and a hand-to-hand fight ensued. Paul fell backwards, knocking over the lamp and the screen. He screamed with pain, hitting his head on the side of the fireplace and causing a deep wound on his forehead. The others, fearing that the shout would be heard, threw themselves on him. Paul tried to get up, but fell back. They were in complete darkness. One could hear cries and groans. Paul managed to push away the hands which were over his mouth. 'Gentlemen, spare me, give me time to pray to Go…' He spoke in French. He did not have time to finish the word God. One of the assailants had undone his scarf and put it round Paul's neck. His groans became a rattle, then stopped. There were a few convulsive movements, then nothing.

When Beningsen came back into the room with a lamp, Paul I was dead. Beningsen had his body carried to the bed. Only then did Pahlen enter the room, sword in hand. He had not wanted to participate in the event he had organized. His treachery, even if it was justified, had made him momentarily weak. At the sight of the corpse, he stopped, the colour left his face, and he leant against the wall. Seemingly drunk with what they had just done and not knowing quite where they were, the conspirators left the dead man's apartment, shouting 'Long live Alexander.' They came face to face with the Empress Maria Feodorovna, who, terrified by what she had heard, was trying to reach her husband. 'Madam, everything is now over. You would uselessly compromise the rest of your days, and those of Paul are over.' The widow cried out and fainted.

Alexander had, for many weeks and months, been in fear of his life and that of his mother. When the conspirators had approached him, he had finally agreed that his father be removed from the throne only to avoid a worse calamity. He had, of course, recommended that they should avoid using violence. The conspirators found him weighed down with grief. 'Oh Pahlen, what a page for the beginning of my history.' The conspirators tried to reason with him. Alexander refused to listen. They had to hustle him into a carriage. As a security measure, Pahlen and Zubov took the place of the footmen at the back of the coach, which set off at a gallop towards the Winter Palace, escorted by Guard battallions. The principal Guard regiments had been gathered on the square by the conspirators. 'Here is the Emperor. Long live the Emperor.' Alexander refused to get down. They pulled him from the coach, pale and defeated. He was dragged along, carried on people's shoulders, and the crowd enthusiastically and sincerely swore him alliegiance, but this popular fervour could not distract the Emperor from his sombre reflexions.

The Summer Garden of the Castle was entirely designed by Paul I. The roof of the Castle can be seen in the background, surmounted by an arrow dedicated to St Michael.

OLD MICHAEL'S
CASTLE

Doctors and surgeons declared that the Emperor Paul had died of apoplexy, but to display the corpse ceremonially in the castle in which he had lived for such a short time, it had to be painted and varnished like a doll. A hat was put on his head to cover the wounds. Bonaparte, learning of this tragic event, imputed that the English had done it. Alexander remained obsessed with his involuntary culpability for the rest of his life. After such a tragedy, no-one in the Imperial family wanted to live in the Castle. It was given to the Engineering School, and as a student, Pushkin wore out the seat of his trousers on its benches. He was to become Russia's greatest poet, and he recalled the castle in one of his poems:

> When the star of midnight twinkles
> On the gloomy waters of the Neva,
> And the head, quite unconcerned,
> Is weighed down with peaceful sleep,
> The pensive poet casts a glance
> At the palace buried in oblivion,
> A tyrant's menacing memorial
> Deserted in the mists of sleep.
>
> And hears the dread voice of Clio
> Above those gloomy walls,
> And sees, as though before his eyes,
> The last hour of Caligula . . .

A. S. Pushkin, Ode: *Freedom*, 1817, ll. 65–76
Trans. Peter Norman

KAMENNOSTROVSKY PALACE

To the north-north-west of St Petersburg, the Neva divides into several tributaries, some wide, some narrow, some quick-flowing and some slow-flowing, creating islands which have for centuries been favourite summer resorts. They are still very charming today: green and romantic, full of undiscovered corners, forgotten monuments and previously grand but now neglected country houses. The most prized of these was Kamennostrovsky, the stone island. Catherine II bought it to build a house for her successor, the future Paul I, aged eight at the time. It was not until 1776 that building work began on the palace, and its architect is not known. The name of Vasili Bazenov, the architect of Old Michael's Castle, has been suggested, but he would have needed help with the building of Kamennostrovsky, and Yuri Velten was probably charged with its execution.

It is a very simple palace, in white and yellow stucco, the favourite colours of the St Petersburgers. On the garden side, a porch lengthened by a staircase descends slowly to the river, the little Nevk. There is an idyllic view over the water which reflects the wooded banks, where here and there one can catch sight of the bell-towers of various monasteries. It is far removed from the huge scale of Tsarskoye Selo or Peterhof, or from the sublime luxury of Pavlovsk. Now a sanatorium for the army, Kamennostrovsky was a real country house. Its most beautiful room, the oval hall, is the only one that has been restored. The same rustic charm is present in the garden, designed by Thomas of Thomon in the purest English style, where the carefully calculated arrangement of lawns, clumps of trees and bowers seems perfectly natural.

After the tragic death of Paul I, who had spent little time there, the palace was inherited by his son and heir, Alexander I, who liked to spend the summer there. It was here that, one day in June 1812, his dusty coach put him down. So much had happened in the few months since he had left St Petersburg. From the beginning of the year, war had been in the air, and the whole of Europe was bristling with rumours that Napoleon was preparing his battle plans. The rumours suggested that he had decided to end his allegiance with Russia, the only continental power that could stand up to him. In Russia they were on tenterhooks, but knew nothing for certain. In April, Napoleon had left Paris for Saxony, which redoubled St Petersburg's anxiety. Alexander had left for Vilnius, in Lithuania, where he had been received like an idol. The Polish magnates had bent over backwards to offer him the most lavish hospitality, and the entire population had acclaimed him, to the sound of bells and canon salvoes proclaiming peace.

They enjoyed themselves so much at Vilnius that some members of St Petersburg society had come to join their Emperor. On 25 July, his aides-de-camp invited him to a grand ball at Zacret, the country house of Beningsen, the man who had assassinated his father. In the middle of a polonaise, a fashionable dance of the time, General Balachev appeared in the ballroom and approached Alexander I. The two men went out onto the terrace. A few minutes later, Alexander returned, pale but perfectly composed, begging to be excused as he had an important matter to attend to. He had just learnt that Napoleon had begun the invasion of Russia. Napoleon advanced with such lightening speed that Alexander had to move his general quarters from Vilnius back to Drissa, then to Moscow. He was received triumphantly, and there, in the old capital, he immersed himself in the vital concerns of the nation.

It was not a time for pomp or festivities, and Alexander liked simplicity. Once back at St Petersburg, he decided to live at Kamennostrovsky for the duration of the war with his wife, Tsarina Elizabeth. This cohabitation marked the couple's reconciliation: they had sincerely loved each other at first but had since grown apart. Alexander had had numerous mistresses whom he suddenly renounced. The bad news continued to arrive. Napoleon had reached Smolensk, one of the most important cities of the Empire – to the Russians' horror, it had gone up in flames. The Imperial family began to panic. Grand Duchess Catherine fled to Yaroslavl; the Empress Dowager, Maria Feodorovna, packed her belongings and withdrew to Kazan. Tsarina Elizabeth showed a fortitude that no one had expected of her. Refusing to run away, this beautiful and neglected woman left her retirement, founded societies to take care of the orphans of war, showed a lively interest in all the organizations which looked after the maimed and wounded, and secretly gave ninety per cent of her civil list to war charities.

Defeat followed on defeat. The generals were divided and could not stop quarrelling. Voices were raised throughout the Empire demanding the return of the old field marshall Kutuzov, the hero of the Turkish wars, and the only one thought capable of saving the Empire. Alexander did not like him but resolved to receive him at Kamennostrovsky on 18 August 1812. On one side of the table sat

KAMENNOSTROVSKY PALACE

This nineteenth-century watercolour of Kamennostrovsky shows its siting on one of the islands in the river Neva just outside St. Petersburg. Catherine II had the Palace built for her son Paul by Yuri Velten, who executed the building from sketches done by Vasili Bazenov.

the veteran, corpulent, blind in one eye, a wily sybarite, tireless, indestructible, adored by the army and knowing Russia and the Russian soul better than anybody. On the other sat the young Tsar, tall and slender, charm itself, soft but impenetrable, who seemed both feminine and, paradoxically, mystical. No one knows exactly what these two said to each other, nor how much of his plans Kutuzov revealed, but in any case he was made commander-in-chief and Alexander, coming out of the meeting, whispered bitterly to a friend close by: 'The public want him in that position, I have put him there, but as far as I am concerned, I wash my hands of him.'

On 10 September, a courier reached Kamennostrovsky with the news that a huge engagement was taking place at Borodino, not far from Moscow. Alexander could not sleep all night. The next morning he received a somewhat optimistic report from Kutuzov, and he thought the battle had been won. The news spread throughout the town. He was acclaimed in the streets. But he soon received a letter from the Governor of Moscow, Count Rostopchin, saying that in spite of the admirable courage shown by the troops, the capital had had to be abandoned. Not only that, but Rostopchin himself had set light to it. Moscow was nothing but a pile of ashes. Alexander cried. The public euphoria turned to consternation, then to indignation and fury. The anniversary of Alexander's crowning fell on the same day. His advisers pleaded with the Tsar not to attend the solemn Te Deum at the cathedral, and his wife begged him at least to use a closed carriage, which he agreed to. The coach rolled slowly through the huge silent crowd which was nothing but a sea of angry faces. Alexander climbed up the steps of the cathedral between two banks of people. Not a single cheer was heard. The only sound was that of his footsteps resonating on the granite steps. For once, he was not able to disguise his feelings, which showed on his face to such an extent that one of the Empress' ladies-in-waiting was so shocked that her knees began to tremble.

Alexander was furious with Kutuzov for having abandoned Moscow. He continued to detest the commander-in-chief, but they were very close in spirit. Whilst his advisers and a part of the Imperial family were encouraging him to negotiate with Napoleon, who was bombarding him with opportunities to do so, he remained entrenched at Kamennostrovsky and refused to give way. There was no question of treaties, or of sueing for peace. Far from weakening him, the defeats and the harrowing loss of Moscow, the burning of the old capital, had only made him more determined. One morning in October, he was rewarded. He received the long-awaited news that, after thirty-two days of occupation, Napoleon had ordered the retreat from Moscow. When Kutuzov heard this, he threw himself at the feet of the icons to thank God, and burst into tears. Alexander had remained impassive, only a thin smile lighting up his drawn face. He was very soon able to take up his peregrinations in reverse, along a road marked out by Russian victories. In December, he entered Vilnius, which he had had to leave in April, where he met up with Kutuzov. He embraced him, made him Prince of Smolensk and pinned on his vast chest the cross of St George, the highest Russian military honour. Between them, but with hardly an idea in common, 'the Greek from the lower Empire', as Napolen had dubbed him and 'the old satyr', as his enemies referred to him, had saved Russia.

The external appearance of the Palace and its gardens has changed little since it was built at the end of the eighteenth century. The river façade has a portico with eight columns and steps which go down almost to the water.

YELAGIN PALACE

WITH the departure of Napoleon for St Helena, the nightmare was over. Peace returned and people were once again able to dedicate their leisure time to pleasure. In 1817 Alexander I bought one of the islands in the Neva, named after its former owner Yelagin, in order to build a palace there for his mother, Maria Feodorovna. He employed Carlo Rossi for his first important project. It was whispered that this son of an Italian ballerina was Tsar Paul's bastard. He had a precocious talent, and had studied in Russia with Vincenzo Brenna, then in Italy. He was young and beautiful, and he single-handedly created a style which was particular to St Petersburg.

The four great modern empires have each left an easily identifiable style as witness to their greatness, each one different from the other. There is the American Imperial style, the British Imperial style, the Austrian Imperial style, and, finally, the Russian Imperial style. The latter is notable for its majesty, its grandiose and disdainful simplicity, and for a cold, proud and inaccessible elegance. When Rossi designed the principal monuments of St Petersburg – the General Quarter facing the Winter Palace, the Senate and the Holy Synod, the Alexander Theatre and the wonderful Theatre Street, now named after him, he characterized the Russian capital by an unreal, fairytale and timeless quality.

To begin with, he built a new summer house for the Dowager Empress. This delicious palace sits amongst the trees on a raised terrace on the edge of the water. All the Russian elements can be found there: the dome, the porticoes, the staircases guarded by marble lions leading down to the lawns. The Queen of St Petersburg, water, can be found everywhere, The interior was decorated with the most luxurious refinement, with the rarest woods and the most delicate marbles adorning the rooms. The mahogany doors were encrusted with gilded bronze, and mythological figures danced gracefully on the polished walls. There are engravings, delicate tints, mirrors, crystal everywhere. Not far from the main house, the kitchens, built in a semi-circle, constitute an extraordinary palace in themselves. The walls are punctuated by niches for statues and vases, just like a neo-classical pavilion. The park was designed by Joseph Bush, the son of the creator of the park at Tsarskoye Selo, and is the most successful in the region round St Petersburg, and it remains the locals' favourite place for walks. Every one of its nooks, each one more inviting than the last, looks like it has been created by one of the Russian landscape painters of the nineteenth century.

Alexander I was always a loving and faithful son, visiting his mother at Yelagin almost every day. She noticed that he was undergoing a profound change. This impenetrable man, who for a long time had been fun-loving, worldly, always wanting to shine in society, had become extremely religious. He

---

The porcelain room. This corner room on the ground floor of the Palace is decorated with white stucco painted with allegorical groups by Antonio Vighi. The entire decoration cost the fabulous sum of 15,000 roubles.

IMPERIAL PALACES OF RUSSIA

had renounced the world and consecrated himself to God. Napoleon's vanquisher, the dominant force in Europe, the soveriegn adored by an entire continent, had never forgotten his father's assassination, and its memory became stronger and more torturing with each day.

One day in 1825, he came to say goodbye to his mother. He was going for a holiday in a remote part of the Crimea in the middle of winter. Soon after, the Empress learned of his inexplicable death. Strange rumours immediately began to fly: the Emperor had arranged for a false death. Maria Feodorovna went as far as Moscow, and for her, and her alone, they opened her son's coffin, which, against normal practice at the time, had already been nailed down. She bent over the coffin and out loud solemnly identified the remains of Tsar Alexander I. Was she telling the truth or was she lying, having previously arranged with her son that she would do this? Was he dead or had he disappeared incognito to become a hermit in Siberia in order to consecrate his life to asking forgiveness from God?

Detail of the stucco-work frieze in the oval hall. The oval hall was designed with sixteen Ionic half-columns, supporting a beautiful cornice. The room's caryatids, decorative groups and bas-reliefs were executed by Stephen Pimenov (1784–1833) and Demuth-Malinovsky.

ABOVE The façade of the Palace, built by Carlo Rossi for Alexander I, overlooking the Neva. FAR LEFT A view of the gardens and stables, a separate compound designed to look like an elegant villa. LEFT Detail of painted stucco work in the porcelain room.

Michael's Palace

ALTHOUGH Yelagin is not small, its design was but a trifle for Rossi. Michael's Palace was a commission more on his scale. Alexander I ordered it for his younger brother, Grand Duke Michael, and Rossi built it between 1819 and 1825. It is a supreme example of the Imperial style which he created – incomparably grand, with obsessive colonnades, an enormously long façade, and an air of classical coldness. In fact, Rossi never designed a building like this without also designing the square in which it would be placed and the neighbouring streets, including their apartment buildings. It was the same for the interior: he never left anything to chance. He designed every detail: the paintings on the walls and ceiling, the marquetry of the parquet flooring, the fireplaces, the chandeliers, the wall brackets and even the furniture. By some extraordinary piece of luck, the white room of Michael's Palace has remained almost completely intact, including the furniture. The sculptures by Mikhail Kozlovsky (1753–1802), the bas-reliefs by Stephan Pimenoff (1784–1833), the frescos by Antonio Vighi (1764–1844), the inordinately ornate and gilded furniture and even the original blue-grey silk hangings still remain and give us a rare example of Imperial decor.

Alexander had been particularly generous with his younger brother, for along with the palace he gave him gold and silver plate, porcelain, glassware and all that was needed not only to live in the palace but also to provide for the large amount of entertaining that was done there.

The Grand Duke had married an extraordinary woman, Helen of Württemberg. She was not only beautiful, intelligent, and cultured, but she also had impressive personality and character. She held the only salon worthy of the name in the capital. She did not retreat into widowhood after the premature death of the Grand Duke in a riding accident while in Warsaw. She was more than liberal, she was humane. She was the first to liberate the serfs in her property at Poltava, creating the first breach in the fabric of the secular system. She did not hide her views, which today would be thought to the left. She received the most liberal ministers, politicians and thinkers. When her brother-in-law Nicholas I rebuked her, she replied: 'It is better for you, Sire, that they speak out loud at my house than conspire in whispers at another's.' She was the source of most of the reforms during the reign that followed, but most of all she had a genius for discovering all kinds of talent. There was no future writer, artist or musician whom she had not entertained. Her house was open to all creative people. For a long time, she was the undisputed queen of St Petersburg society, a grand lady in the old style, noble and proud, who looked down at the world from her throne, but who was never petty or vengeful.

A detail of the main staircase of Michael's Palace: a gallery punctuated by classical figures.

IMPERIAL PALACES OF RUSSIA

Today Michael's Palace is the home of the Russian Museum. In spite of what one might think, the Museum was created before the Revolution. At the end of the last century, Alexander III, the great Russophile, began to buy paintings from collectors or directly from Russian artists, and his residence was soon unable to hold his collection. He considered opening a museum, but died before he could do so. His son and successor, Nicholas II, was quick to complete the project. The Crown bought Michael's Palace, which now displays some of the world's most wonderful icons, charming eighteenth-century portraits, romantic nineteenth-century landscapes, the fairytale fantasies of the great scenic designers of the Russian ballet and masterpieces of the modern Russian school, so little known elsewhere.

The white hall. This room is one of the few of all the Imperial Palaces to retain its original decor and furniture. The furniture was also designed by Carlo Rossi, and the frescoes were commissioned from Antonio Vighi.

Detail of the gate and façade colonnading of the Palace. The building, by Carlo Rossi, is a triumph of Imperial Russian style – majestic both in its scale and its sobriety.

Michael's Palace, nineteenth-century colour lithograph drawn by J. Charlemagne. The Palace was built between 1819 and 1825 for Grand Duke Michael, Alexander I's younger brother. Nicholas II later transformed the Palace into the Russian Museum, dedicated to the arts of his country.

Peterhof Cottage

AS the nineteenth century progressed, the Imperial family became more and more bourgeois in its mentality, lifestyle and the decor it adopted for its houses. Having worked its way slowly up the social ladder, the bourgeoisie had become the dominant class. It no longer tried to imitate the eighteenth-century aristocracy; now, it was the aristocracy and even royalty that imitated them. The Tsars, who had once been geniuses, monsters or eccentrics, were now bourgeois. Another factor in this transformation, and closely linked to it, was the Germanization of the ruling family. Nicholas I, the brother and successor to Alexander I, had a German parent, as well as German grandparents and great-grandparents. Like all his brothers, he had married a German Princess, Charlotte of Prussia, who became the Empress Alexandra Feodorovna. These two elements combine perfectly in the Peterhof 'Cottage'.

The Tsarina hated the pomp of the Great Palace of Peter I, and asked her husband to provide a more intimate family house. To please her, Nicholas built the Cottage, using his English architect Adam Menelaws (1753–1831). From afar, it looks like a gingerbread house. As one approaches, one finds an over-elaborate pavilion with quantities of balconies, verandas and stained glass. Inside, albeit unconciously, it is triumphantly Victorian, even though the Russian dynasty hated the Queen of England. The place is full of family portraits, busts, photographs, trinkets and souvenirs. In contrast to generations of Tsars, Nicholas I and his wife were not seeking beauty and luxury, but aimed more for comfort and, even worse, cosiness. Life at the Cottage was essentially a middle-class family life of Mummy, Daddy and the children. There was no protocol; simplicity and good-natured fun reigned in a setting that called for it. Peterhof had become a resort for retired people and for the middle-classes, the *dachnikis* or owners of *dachas*. Even the Tsar himself was a sort of *dachnik* in his cottage. Nobody stood on ceremony at Peterhof. When they went out, the Grand Duchesses sometimes came across soldiers from the nearby barracks who were swimming naked in the canal or river. As the Imperial coaches approached, the soldiers were seized with panic. Taken by surprise, the men rushed out of the water, not to get their clothes but to thrust their hats on, and in this strange attire, their hair dripping wet, they would stand to attention.

The Marquis of Custine was an exceptional witness of the period. He came from a great French family, but had had to go into exile after a scandal. He left an incisive and very vivid account of Russia. He dearly wanted to visit the cottage at Peterhof, but his friend and guide, Madame X, explained to him the

---

A detail of the Cottage, showing its 'Hansel and Gretel' like appearance. The Imperial family, although Russian in spirit, was now one hundred per cent German by blood.

IMPERIAL PALACES OF RUSSIA

ABOVE The large study, also shown in the watercolour on page 136. The furniture has been changed to heavy neo-Gothic pieces, but the decoration of the cornices and the paintings hung in the room remain.

RIGHT The staircase on the top floor of the Cottage. The 'Gothic' wallpaper, with its perspectives between the columns, is a masterpiece of its kind.

IMPERIAL PALACES OF RUSSIA

insurmountable difficulties of such a project, especially when the Imperial family were in residence. He extended his visit solely in order to wait for the departure of the Cottage's inhabitants, so that he might quietly slip in and have a look around. One day, Madame X came to fetch him at a quarter to eleven, to take him round the Cottage while the Emperor and Empress were out for a walk. Custine, trembling with excitement, arrived at the cottage: 'A small house which they had built in the middle of the noble park of Peterhof, in the new Gothic style so much in vogue in England.'

Tall trees shaded the house, which was surrounded with flowers. It reminded him of other cottages he had seen in London, near Twickenham, on the banks of the Thames. With Madame X acting as guide, he went into the hall and had just had time to examine the furniture of one drawing room, which he found too elaborate, when a valet rushed up and whispered a few words in the ear of his guide, who seemed shocked. 'The Empress has returned.' 'How unfair, I will not have time to see anything.' Alexandra Feodorovna (formerly Charlotte of Prussia) appeared, veiled and dressed all in white. He bowed and kissed her hand. 'Her eyes had a look of gentleness and melancholy.' Custine had heard that she was a haughty woman, who was always ill, but nothing could equal the grace of her welcome. She admitted to having shortened her walk because she had learned from Madame X that he was coming and she wanted at all costs to

Colour lithograph by J. Meyer, showing the Cottage as it was when used as an Imperial residence under Nicholas I. The Tsar arrives in his barouche on a glorious summer day.

meet him. Custine mumbled some words of gratitude. The Empress spoke about the Cottage:

PETERHOF COTTAGE

> I find the residence at Peterhof unbearable, and it was to relieve my eyes from the glare of all that massive gold that I begged the Emperor to build me this house. But now that one of my daughters is married and that my sons are pursuing their studies elsewhere, it has become too large for us.

This modest house was too large for them, who owned the biggest palaces in the world. However, this confession could only please Custine, who let himself be charmed by the Empress, perhaps also because the attention she was paying him appealed to his snobbery.

Alexandra Feodorovna put her eldest son in charge of Custine, with instructions to show him the whole house. He visited everything, even the Grand Duchesses' bedrooms, examining every detail with the avidity of a peeping Tom. He found it rich and elegant, but without a single object or painting of any real artistic worth. Perhaps the valuable masterpieces had been removed from this modest setting. In spite of this, if one likes art, remarked Custine, one puts it everwhere, because one cannot do without it. But here it was not the principal preoccupation of the inhabitants. He found the Grand

A general view of the intimate Peterhof Cottage.

135

IMPERIAL PALACES OF RUSSIA

Drawing room of Empress Alexandra Feodorovna, nineteenth-century watercolour. In such a domestic setting the Empress felt at ease. Through the bay window of this room she had a marvellous view of the Baltic.

The large study, nineteenth-century watercolour by E. G. Hau. By the second half of the nineteenth century, the Imperial family were adopting middle-class German fashions, and preferred the cosy proportions of the Cottage to their grand palaces.

PETERHOF
COTTAGE

Duke's presence inhibiting, and he did not want to show his timidity, because he knew that nothing annoyed royals more. The young heir seemed to sense the visitor's feelings, for he suddenly abandoned him, leaving Madame X to do the honours. Right at the top of the house, under the eaves, Custine found Nicholas I's study:

> A tolerably large and very simple library opening onto a balcony which overlooks the sea. Without leaving this watchtower, the Emperor can give orders to his fleet. For this purpose, he has a spy glass, a speaking trumpet and a little telegraph which he can operate himself.

Custine returned to the Empress, who was among her cherished flowers. He thanked her effusively, which she graciously acknowledged, kissed her hand and bowed. The visit was over.

Within the vast Imperial domain of Peterhof, villas the size of huge chateaux started to spring up here and there in the nineteenth century to house the numerous relatives of the Tsar. His third son, Grand Duke Nicholas, liked to spend his holidays in a delightful seventeenth-century mansion (now an old people's home), to which he added enormous stables in the same architectural style, such that they constituted a palace in themselves. The stables are now abandoned and stand romantically amongst the trees on the banks of a dark pond. The Duke of Leuchtenberg, related by marriage to Nicholas I, received one of the most extraordinary houses built by the architect Andrei Stakenschneider: a neo-Classical villa. Its porticoes, atria, urns, roof terraces and pools, all the usual paraphernalia of the Mediterranean shores, appear quite exotic under the low and threatening skies of the Baltic.

Two exterior views of the Palace of Grand Duke Nicholas, outside St Petersburg: ABOVE an overall view of the vast stable buildings; BELOW a detail of the façade of the Palace.

PETERHOF
COTTAGE

139

PETERHOF
COTTAGE

Two views of the Palace of the Duke of Leuchtenberg, now an appealing neo-Greek ruin. It was built by Andrei Stackenschneider in the grounds of Peterhof Palace, and its Greek revival architecture is unique in Russia.

The Winter Palace under Nicholas I and Alexander II

NE evening in December 1837, when Tsar Nicholas I was attending the Theatre Marie, he was brought the news that the Winter Palace was on fire. He rushed to the scene, but by the time he arrived, the palace was nothing but a ball of fire, the flames reaching up into the sky. Its art treasures, the paintings of the Hermitage, were only saved thanks to the heroic efforts of the soldiers and firemen, several of whom lost their lives. When the fire was finally put out, the entire interior was nothing but ashes.

Nicholas I was not easily discouraged. He immediately engaged the services of the architect Vasili Stasov. A pupil of Vasili Bazenov, he had already worked at Oranienbaum, at Peterhof and at Tsarskoye Selo. The works were carried out the Russian way, that is to say briskly. Twenty thousand roubles were invested in the site in one year. Even the winter did not stop the labourers, and in the worst frosts, fires were permanently lit to prevent the materials from freezing, by order of the Tsar. The Russians like to finish what they have begun, and the Winter Palace had recovered its youth within two years.

Stasov could have put his own mark and style on the palace, but his great soul and great talent led him first and foremost to respect the work of his predecessors, and he faithfully restored it. Everything returned to its original state: the Jordan staircase, the Rastrelli chapel, Rossi's military gallery which Alexander I had commissioned in order to commemorate the war of 1812 (and which he had filled with portraits of his heroes painted by the Englishman, George Dawe, 1781–1829), the little throne room by Auguste Richard de Montferrand (1786–1858), St George's Hall, begun by Rastrelli and finished by Quarenghi. Prudently, Stasov took out the splendid, magnificently decorated ceramic stoves, which were a constant fire hazard, and replaced them with hot air pipes.

Nicholas I also left his own contribution to the Winter Palace. The man who was to become his favourite architect, the German Andrei Stakenschneider, created for him the pavilion room. Full of marvels, this suspended garden occupies the entire centre of the little Hermitage. Stakenschneider created an oriental wonderland, still in existence: an incomparable symphony of crystals, marbles, fountains, mosaics, hard stone, gilt, which transports the visitor away

---

The magnificent gilded staircase of the Winter Palace.

from the cold North. Nicholas I's study no longer exists in its original state. It was, however, a remarkable manifestation of its occupant's austere personality. A room of modest proportions, with a vaulted ceiling, no decoration and functional furniture, it has the look of a soldier-monk's cell.

In contrast, Nicholas I wanted great luxury for his wife, Alexandra. Stasov and his pupil Alexander Bryullov (1798–1877) designed the malachite room as her private drawing room. During the previous century, they had discovered mines of this semi-precious stone in the Urals, and it had since become the decorative trademark of the Russian Imperial family. In the same way that those immediately recognizable vast Sèvres vases signal a gift from a French regime, a trinket in malachite, usually enormous, always indicates a gift from the Tsar.

At the time of the Tsarina Alexandra, her drawing room was a triumph of plush. Now only the malachite and the gilt remain. The green stone can be found in the columns, the pilasters, the huge bowl supported by gilded bronze figures, the torchères, the vases. Gilt covered the rest. Green and gold, sumptuous, delicate, this room still remains today a symbol of Imperial luxury. In the Empress' bedroom, showcases as big as Normandy wardrobes were lined up along the walls, in which, as was the custom, her jewels were displayed. Each one contained several complete sets of diamonds, emeralds, rubies, sapphires, turquoises and pearls, for the taste for elaborate jewellery had never been as great. When, for example, Nicholas I's sister, Anna Pavlovna, the Queen of Holland, watched hers go up in flames when her palace burnt down, her brother rushed to send her replacements. In the Winter Palace there was also the diamond room, opened only for certain high-ranking visitors, where the state jewels were exhibited: crowns, sceptres, clasps, globes, all resplendent with diamonds.

Alexandra Feodorovna's boudoir was also restored by Alexander Bryullov, then entirely redecorated by Stakenschneider, who transformed it into the dazzling example of red and gold nineteenth-century roccoco which still exists today. Her previous boudoir from before the fire held too many bad memories for the Empress. She had never forgotten that very frightening day of 14 December 1825. The Empire had been without a Tsar for almost three weeks. Alexander was or was not dead in far away Crimea. His immediate successor, Constantin, did not want to reign and had designated his younger brother Nicholas as successor. Even though the two brothers were in perfect agreement, complete political and constitutional confusion reigned. Finally, on this 14 December, the crisis seemed resolved, and the authorities were about to swear alliegiance to the new Emperor Nicholas I. However, rumours had reached him of an imminent military uprising. At eleven o'clock the Court, the authorities and the officers of the garrison gathered at the palace for a solemn Te Deum. At that moment, the worst possible news began to circulate. One by one, the regiments were beginning to mutiny. The Empress Alexandra wrote:

Detail of the exterior of the 'New Hermitage', built next to the Winter Palace by Nicholas I as a museum where visitors could admire the Imperial collections. It was built by the architect Leo von Klenze (1784–1864), and the picture shows its most famous external decoration – one of the statues supporting the porch.

I was alone at midday when Nicholas came into my room saying that I must go. I could tell from his voice that the news was bad. I knew he did not intend to leave the palace. It gave me a shock. I went on with the business of dressing, for at two o'clock we had to be ready for the state procession for the Te Deum. Suddenly, the door opened and the Dowager Empress appeared, her face haggard. 'Darling,' she said to me, 'things are going very badly.' Deathly pale and unable to say a word, I threw a shawl on to cover my shoulders and went with the Dowager Empress to her small study. From there, we could see that the whole square in front of the palace was full of people. We knew nothing. All we had heard was that the Moscow regiment had rebelled.

THE WINTER PALACE UNDER NICHOLAS I AND ALEXANDER II

Nicholas began by putting the palace on a war footing: the guards were put in a state of alert, the great door was closed. Aides-de-camp and officers were sent in every direction to the barracks in the town. In the square, the crowd of spectators who had come for the Te Deum grew by the minute. The rebellious regiments had placed themselves in front of the Senate. Following his instincts and refusing to listen to his wife's or his counsellors' supplications, Nicholas decided to go out. He put the loyal soldiers of the Peobrazensky regiment in charge of his family. An extraordinary sight was waiting for him outside the palace. Dressed in their gala uniforms, the insurgents had formed a square around the huge crowd of onlookers. Between them and Nicholas symbolically stood Falconet's statue of Peter the Great. The ambassadors, anxious to see the spectacle, had rushed forward, but Nicholas sent them away. 'This scene is a family affair which has nothing to do with Europe.' The diplomats did not need telling twice.

More newly-mutinous regiments poured into the square and formed another square of a thousand men. At that moment, the Archbishop of St Petersburg appeared at the head of the clergy who were carrying holy icons. He tried to exhort the rebels to see reason. They responded to him with insults. As time went on, the situation became more and more threatening, but Nicholas could not bring himself to give the order to shoot. Russians could not kill other Russians. Not once did he lose his head – he remained extremely pale, but calm. He hesitated. Finally, he decided to have four cannons brought onto the square. He gave the order to fire twice, and twice he countermanded it. Suddenly the guns of the loyal regiments went off, without anyone ever knowing who had given the order. The insurgents panicked at once. Inside the palace, the Empress thought she would go mad.

From what we could see of the movements of the troops, we knew that there was shooting. I knew that the life most precious to me was in danger. We felt as if we were dying. We constantly sent messengers, but none of them returned. The few witnesses to what was happening thought that the Emperor was being too patient. They admired his calm, his composure and gentleness, but wished he would decide more quickly on energetic action and use the

---

The malachite room, the work of Vasili Stasov, who restored the Palace after a fire in 1836. Malachite had recently been discovered in the Urals and became so fashionable that this room was dominated by its use.

army, but I understood so well what my Nicholas was feeling in his heart. When I heard the first salvo, I fell on my knees. My little boys were beside me in my study. Oh, how I prayed. I have never prayed like that before. I had seen Russian blood being shed by Russians.

Nicholas only returned to the Winter Palace at six o'clock in the evening after the rebellion had been crushed. Meanwhile, in the chapel, the Court was still waiting for the Te Deum without quite knowing what was going on outside. Night had fallen when the royal couple finally appeared. The Empress had not had time to change. Among the gala uniforms and sparkling Court dresses, she wore a simple little morning dress and held on tightly to her husband's arm.

Nicholas did not understand how men could want to take his life and overthrow the regime. He had the rebels brought to the Winter Palace to follow their interrogation closely, and often intervened personally. These terrible sessions paradoxically took place in the most sumptuous decor in the world, that of the Hermitage, amongst the mahogany doors, encrusted with precious woods, the fireplaces in gilded bronze, the gigantic vases in lapis lazuli, porphyry, jaspar and malachite. Under the domed and decorated ceilings, surrounded by brocade and silk, the men who had risked everything for their ideals played for their lives in front of the Tsar, who refused to understand.

Everyone thought that the Empress Alexandra Feodorovna held her Court admirably. She liked entertaining, and she knew her world well. She mixed dignity with affability, and although she did not possess her mother's beauty, the incomparable Louise of Prussia, she had inherited her grace. Under her rule, the Court shone brilliantly. The first ball of the year took place on 10 January. In the social life jargon of the time it would be called 'washday'. It was not a very elegant reunion because far too many people had to be invited: the first four ranks of the 'Chins', the administrative ranks, the members of the Imperial household, right down to former ladies-in-waiting, and many others. Seven or eight thousand invitations were sent out. The most unexpected people came: the provincials travelling for the occasion from their distant districts; the eccentric governors of the regions; civil servants who, according to the snobs, would not have been admitted into a fashionable salon. The guests arrived at eight-thirty and entered the palace by different entrances according to their rank. The whole Winter Palace was brilliantly lit. Inside everything was resplendent. One hundred thousand candles were needed for one night. Braziers burned around Alexander's column. The coaches followed each other at walking pace. The women got out at the portals and teetered about on tiptoes to avoid putting their feet in the snow. Fur of every kind could be seen: sable, chinchilla, mink. They wore no shawls on their heads so as not to disturb the arrangement of their tiaras. Coats were handed to the Court valets, who wrapped them up straight away and pinned on the owner's visiting card. The guests would slowly mount the great Jordan staircase covered with thick red carpet. The ladies of the Court

---

The throne room, conceived as a homage to Peter the Great. His portrait was painted by the Venetian Nicolò Miconi (1650–1730) five years after his death. The throne, made by Nicholas Clausen, a French protestant escaped to London, is decorated in silver gilt and with Imperial motifs, which are echoed as decorative elements of the ceiling.

all wore traditional costume, a dark velvet dress in red, blue or green, worn over a white satin skirt, and a train embroidered with flowers and gold and silver leaves. In their hair they wore the *kakoshnik*, a kind of cloth diadem onto which were sewn enormous precious stones. They all sported either the Imperial monogram in diamonds or the portrait of the Emperor surrounded by diamonds and attached by a ribbon. The mounted guards wore red, white and gold uniforms, silver breast-plates and helmets crowned with the Imperial eagle. The Emperor's Circassian Guards wore blue caftans covered with rows of silver cartridge cases. The Cossack officers, their trousers tucked into their black boots, wore green tunics with white silk belts. The Court functionaries had frock-coats decorated with wide bands of gold. Some of the foreigners were equally magnificent: the Hungarian ambassador of the Austrian Empire and the Polish magnates were resplendent in their national costumes.

The flood of guests increased by the minute. They filed between two rows of Cossack Guards in red uniforms and gigantic negroes with turbans, a gift from the Negus. The grand master of ceremonies, his long ebony cane with its ivory handle in his hand, greeted them and directed them to the drawing rooms. Suddenly, the orchestra struck up a very slow march. The grand master struck the floor three times. The Abyssinians opened the doors to the malachite drawing room and all eyes turned in that direction. The Imperial family appeared. The Emperor was in uniform, the Empress covered in so many diamonds that she appeared to be one big stone, the big blue sash of St Andrew crossing her white satin dress. The Grand Duchesses followed, covered with an almost equal number of precious stones.

The ball started with a Court Polonaise, a kind of slow rhythmic procession around the Nicholas hall, the Tsar giving his hand to the wife of the doyen of the diplomatic corps. A waltz followed. If one of the Grand Duchesses wanted to dance, she would send her equerry to invite the partner of her choice. Lackeys passed through the crowd offering refreshments and ices. In the neighbouring rooms one could see champagne being cooled in enormous blocks of ice. *Petits-fours*, cakes and other delicacies were passed round, masterpieces from the famous palace confectioners. At the appointed time, the master of ceremonies opened the way for their majesties, who proceeded to the supper room. Even though it was mid-winter, rare and expensive spring and summer produce was brought in fresh from the Crimea or from the South of France. The phrase coined to explain the splendours of the ball became: 'My dear, there was fresh asparagus for everybody.' A caustic commentator added: 'There might have been asparagus for everybody, but there certainly was not enough room for this very mixed assembly and the crush was greater than anything that could be imagined. There was hardly elbow room, and to enjoy oneself was quite out of the question.'

The supper over, the Emperor took the Empress back into the Nicholas hall where the cotillion began. While their guests twirled, the Imperial couple slipped quietly away, their duty done.

The Empress was then free to receive her friends. She would do this four times during the winter, giving what were known as the 'Palm Balls' which took place in the concert hall of the Winter Palace. For these, a hundred palms were brought from the greenhouses at Tsarkoye Selo and placed in the middle of supper tables which could seat twelve. A bed of roses would be spread around each trunk. The Empress' table would be raised above another bed of tulips and jonquils, where she would receive the Grand Duchesses and the ambassadors. The Emperor did not sit down. He would move from table to table, talking to his guests. At each one, he would take a small piece of bread, a piece of fruit and sip a glass of champagne so that each one would be able to say that they had dined with the sovereign. These sumptuous yet elegant gatherings, encounters between accomplices in an enchanted and inaccessible universe, marked the triumph of a supremely refined society.

In fact, the Empress rarely appeared at these balls. It was no longer Alexandra Feodorovna but her successor, Maria Alexandrovna, who attended them. When Alexander II was still only the heir to the throne, he had fallen madly in love with her during a visit to Darmstadt. In spite of the doubtful legitimacy of this young Princess of Hesse, and his parents' objections, he had persevered and had finally succeeded in marrying her. Maria Alexandrovna was popular neither with royalty nor with Russian society. She was thought to be cold, and much too attached to protocol, niggling over details. She never got over the death at twenty-two of her eldest son Nicholas in a riding accident. Towards the end, she was affected by tuberculosis and the rooms of her apartment were continually fed with oxygen supplied by cylinders, which gave her ladies-in-waiting violent migraines. She was a profoundly unhappy woman, for the whole of Russia knew that her husband came to love another woman.

The Princess Catherine Dolgoruky, Katya to her friends, was a ravishing adolescent, freshly out of the Institute of Smolny where noble young ladies were educated. One day, when crossing the Summer Garden, she came across Alexander II who was taking his daily walk, followed by his aide-de-camp. He had known her since childhood, so observers were not surprised when he greeted her, but they were considerably surprised to see him drag the young girl into a quiet alley. They met again, but Katya did not want to listen. Slowly, she changed. One day, Alexander appeared so unhappy , so alone, that she did not want to see him go. When she saw him the next time, she later said that she experienced a change of heart, like a blow in the chest. Her surrender was close. It took place in July 1866, when the Court was at Peterhof, in a pavilion of the Belvedere. The Tsar promised to marry her one day. They feverishly pursued their passionate liaison for years, and it was crowned with the birth of three children. Alexander no longer hid his passion and the dying Empress could hear her rival's bastards running and jumping in the room exactly above hers. She finally died and Alexander II immediately fulfilled his promise and married Katya, to whom he had given the title Princess Yurievskaya. And as happiness is contagious, he prepared to give the Empire a constitution which would slowly transform it from an absolute to a parliamentary monarchy. So everything was for the best in the best of all possible worlds , when one day, Sunday 1 March 1881, as his grandson, the future Nicholas II who was his favourite, recounted:

> We were at lunch in the Anichkov Palace, my brother and I, when a frightened servant ran to tell us that a misfortune had befallen the Emperor. 'The Tsarevich (Alexander III) has given orders for the Grand Duke Nicholas Alexandrovich to go immediately to the Winter Palace. He must take the first

convenient means of transport, no time is to be lost.' General Danilov and we two hurried downstairs and got into a Court carriage, which was waiting for somebody. We drove down the Nevsky at top speed to the Winter Palace. As we went up the stairs, I saw pale faces everywhere. On the carpet, there were deep red stains. My grandfather was bleeding to death from his terrible wounds as he was carried upstairs.

It was a nihilist assassination attempt. A bomb had been thrown at the Tsar's carriage.

In his study, I found my parents, and my uncles and aunts were standing by the window. No one spoke. My grandfather was lying on the narrow camp-bed he always slept in. He was covered by the military coat he used as a dressing-gown. His face was deathly pale. There were small wounds all over it. His eyes were closed. My father led me up to the bed. 'Papa,' he said, raising his voice, 'your sunshine is here.' I saw the flicker of an eyelid. Grandfather's blue eyes opened and he tried to smile.

At that moment, Katya rushed into the room, half-dressed, and threw herself on her lover's bed, kissing his hands and crying 'Sasha, Sasha'. It was unbearable. The Grand Duchesses began to cry. 'Silence,' cried out a voice, 'the end is near.' The Court chaplain administered the last rites. The Tsar's fixed look became cloudy. 'The Emperor is dead,' cried out the Court doctor. Princess Yurievskaya let out a single cry and dropped to the floor like a felled tree. Her pink and white négligé was drenched in blood. Two guards carried her to her apartment while the doctors began to dress the body of Alexander II.

Exterior detail of the Winter Palace, including the watch tower from which messages could be sent.

Strelna

THE tragic death of Alexander II also provoked the disgrace of his brother, Grand Duke Constantin, who had pushed him hard in the direction of his liberal reforms. The new Emperor, Alexander III, an out and out conservative, made his uncle understand that he no longer had a place in the affairs of the Empire, or even of the capital. The uncle was retired, almost forcibly, to the country. He owned the palace at Pavlovsk, but he also spent a lot of time at his other residence, the castle at Strelna. It was built in 1711 on the road between the capital and Peterhof by the French architect Alexandre Le Blond for Peter the Great. The exterior was left intact but the interior was almost completely remodelled in the nineteenth century by Grand Duke Contantin. He had been named Viceroy of Poland by his brother Alexander II, and with his liberalism and generosity he succeeded in being the only Russian occupier who, if not loved, was at least tolerated by the Poles. His fall from grace darkened his character. He brooded over the failure of the dream that he and Alexander II had conceived. He had married Princess Alexandra of Saxe-Alterburg, a renowned beauty so proud of her appearance that even when she was very old she slept in

LEFT Nineteenth-century watercolour of the Palace, which at the time belonged to Grand Duke Constantine Nicholaevich, Alexander II's brother.
RIGHT View of the façade of the Palace, built by Alexandre Le Blond in 1711 for Peter the Great, and of its gardens reaching to the Baltic.

a corset to keep her waist small and had ivory paper knives made in the shape of her tiny foot to give to her friends.

One of their daughters, Olga, became Queen of Greece, and one of their sons, Constantin Contantinovich became a writer of repute. He translated Shakespeare into Russian, left numerous poems and several plays, one of which, *The King Of Judea*, was a great success. He even took to the boards himself. He died during the First World War, in 1915, and his solemn funeral was the last great Imperial ceremony before the Revolution.

Strelna was a sumptuous resort. It had many Russian paintings, but also some very good Italian and Flemish pictures, including a Salvator Rosa and a Philip Wouwerman. The ballroom was magnificent; it was literally covered in mirrors, and its ornamental ceiling was hung with a large number of beautiful chandeliers. In the garden, the view extended across lawns and canals lined with great trees all the way to the Gulf of Finland. Today, on the road to Peterhof, one can glimpse between the jungle of fully-grown trees the great yellow and white carcass of the newly repainted palace, but when one approaches, one has the heart-breaking sight of a masterpiece threatened with ruin. The park has returned to nature, but one can still distinguish its outline.

Marinsky Palace

OF all his children, Nicholas I by far preferred his eldest daughter, Grand Duchess Maria Nikolayevna. He asked his dear Stakenschneider to build her a palace worthy of this favouritism. The architect, who was responsible for many more palaces which we shall visit, began in 1844. He built an immense residence opposite the new St Isaac's Cathedral, entirely in the Imperial style which was then fashionable. In front of the palace was placed a bronze statue of Nicholas I, in armour and helmet, on a prancing horse. The pedestal features bronze beauties representing his virtues, whose faces are those of his wife and four daughters.

Maria Nikolayevna had married the Duke of Leuchtenberg, whose family had an interesting past. The Empress Josephine had two sons by her first marriage, one of whom, Eugene, had been made Viceroy of Italy by Napoleon. He married the daughter of the King of Bavaria, which not only gave him the title of Leuchtenberg but more importantly enabled him to be the only one of the Imperial clan to survive their destruction, the King of Bavaria having taken charge of his son-in-law. In the next generation, the Duke of Leuchtenberg married the daughter of the Tsar, whose father did not want to be separated from her. He then Russianized himself, and he and his descendents became a part of the Imperial family, giving himself a second unexpected chance. The 1917 Revolution put a stop to this state of grace, but the Leuchtenbergs, who had more than one card in their hand, rediscovered their Bavarian possessions and escaped from disaster a third time. Nicholas I never knew what his favourite daughter took pains to hide from him: when she was widowed, she fell in love with a Count Strogonov, whom she had the unimaginable audacity to marry secretly. At her death, her palace became the seat of the Imperial Council, the highest body in Imperial Russia. Today, it is the seat of the municipal council of St Petersburg.

The internal decoration has quite a few remains of its original splendour: the monumental staircase; the central colonnaded rotunda, lengthened by what was to have been a winter garden; the central drawing room which looks out on Marinsky Square, with its rich doors in precious wood encrusted with rare metals; the Grand Duchess Maria's private apartments which still retain a very personal atmosphere, although they have lost all their furniture; and lastly, almost under the eaves, her recently restored private chapel, painted with pseudo-Byzantine frescos, the work of a little-talented Prince Gagarin.

The red drawing room, the most sumptuous room of the Palace. Its famous doors are the most elaborate in all the Russian palaces. Made of mahogany, inlaid with ivory, mother-of-pearl and precious metals, they are rather the work of a jeweller than a carpenter.

TOP Detail of the recently restored chapel, situated on the top floor of the Palace. ABOVE Nineteenth-century colour lithograph of the Palace as it was built by Nicholas I for his favourite daughter, Maria, Duchess of Leuchtenberg. RIGHT The rotunda, lit from its glass ceiling – one of the architect Andrei Stakenschneider's masterpieces.

OVERLEAF Detail of the rotunda room, decorated in the fragile Pompeian fashion which survived in Russia up to the middle of the nineteenth century.

Grand Duke Nicholas' Palace

The city of St Petersburg was expanding and new districts were being created, particularly to the west of the Admiralty. It was here that in 1862 Andrei Stakenschneider finished a huge residence destined for the third son of Nicholas I, Grand Duke Nicholas Nikolayevich. The architect abandoned the neo-classicism he had perhaps been forced to employ. His real temperament led him towards an over-ornate Italian style, of which this palace is one of many examples.

Grand Duke Nicholas was a very handsome man, whom many thought of as 'inexpressibly stupid although he considers himself clever'. His shining hour came in the Crimean War, and then, even more so, in the Russo-Turkish war of 1877 where, popular with the army, he was commander-in-chief. On the death of his brother Alexander II, he was pushed into obscurity, for his nephew Alexander III did not approve of his private life. He had married a princess of Oldenburg, but in reality led two lives and had two homes. He had for many years been in love with Ekaterina Shislova, by whom he had had several children. The lady's exigencies and Nicholas' spendthrift habits put him into such financial difficulty that he had to sell Stakenschneider's palace and retire to the Crimea. There he quietly waited for his wife to die so that he could marry his mistress. But as so often happens in these cases, it was the mistress who died first, and the wife even survived her husband.

Several main rooms of the palace have kept their sumptuous decor, particularly the entrance hall with the marble staircase lined with columns, serveral rococo drawings rooms of the mid-nineteenth century, and a Moorish boudoir. Today, the Grand Duke's home has become a 'Palace of Work', where, in the magnificent Stakenschenider decor, gifts from trade unions from all over the world to their brothers in Russia are displayed. A more sensationally ugly collection of objects is hard to imagine.

The grandson of Nicholas, who bore the same name and was the most famous of that branch of the family, became a rather successful commander-in-chief of the Imperial armies at the beginning of the First World War. He subsequently built himself a palace near the humble hut of his ancestor, the founder of St Petersburg, Peter the Great. The imposing dwelling is crowned by a huge dome in green bronze, and has since been converted into a wedding house for public use.

Built for Nicholas I's son, Grand Duke Nicholas, this Palace is another example of Stakenschneider's Italianate style.

Top Grand Duke Nicholas Nicholaevich's Palace was built in a new district which was being developed to the west of St Petersburg.

Above Detail of the marquetry wood panelling in the Moorish smoking room. As was the fashion also in other parts of Europe, gentlemen would retire here to smoke.

Left The staircase is certainly the most sumptuous element of the Palace, with its double turn, colonnades and vast stairwell made up of numerous different marbles.

IMPERIAL PALACES OF RUSSIA

NEW MICHAEL'S PALACE

ON the Winter Quay, which lies alongside the palace of the same name, and which also passes in front of so many sumptuous palaces, the Crown owned several buildings facing the Peter and Paul fortress on land which they had bought from Count Cheremetiev. In 1863 it was again Andrei Stakenschneider who brought these buildings together in his inimitable style to create a palace for the fourth son of Nicholas I, Grand Duke Michael Nicholayevich.

Vaguely in the Florentine style, or possibly indeterminate Italian style, the exterior and interior of the palace remain the most striking example of the German architect's penchant for sumptuousness. Over-ornate, over-gilded, in the eyes of some it could be thought of as verging on bad taste. Columns, stucco and marbles can be found everywhere, which at the time would have been complemented by Spanish leather on the walls, parquet floors made of rare woods, and very gilded furniture. 'Rather Victorian-looking and stiff,' according to one of the Grand Duchesses who lived there.

The palace was so vast that one of the sons of the house, Sergei Michailovich, used to borrow a bicycle to cross the rooms to visit his sister-in-law. Grand Duke Michael had been named Governor in the Caucasus, and he took straight away to this very picturesque and still wild region. He stayed there nineteen years, adapting to the local customs and slowly, with constant efforts, integrated this profoundly independent province into the Empire. He was deeply in love with his wife, the Grand Duchess Olga Feodorovna, born Princess of Bade, an intelligent woman, hard-headed and critical, and above all very authoritarian. When she learned that her son Michael had secretly married a woman not his equal, evidently without her permission, she had a heart attack and died in a provincial station.

Grand Duke Michael's sons were mostly irreverent, liberal and open. Nicholas became an historian. Imprisoned during the Revolution, Gorky in person asked for his pardon from Lenin, who replied: 'The Revolution does not need historians.' And like so many of his family, he was shot.

Andrei Stakenschneider designed this residence on the banks of the Neva in his characteristic Italian style for Nicholas I's youngest son, Grand Duke Michael.

166

Gatchina Palace

AFTER the assassination of Alexander II, and with anarchists and nihilists infiltrating everywhere in Russia, as everywhere else in Europe, it was thought advisable that the Emperor no longer reside in the capital. But where was he to live? He hated Tsarskoye Selo as it was there that he had witnessed the ten year reign of his father's mistress, Princess Yurievskaya. Peterhof was uninhabitable in the winter. The choice fell on Gatchina. It was a distant palace, 80 kilometres south of St Petersburg, isolated and therefore easier to protect.

In 1766 Antonio Rinaldi had been commanded by Catherine II to build a country residence for her lover Grigory Orlov. On his death, she had bought it back and given it to her son Paul I, who had considerably 'improved' the palace. It now had nine hundred rooms. It consisted of two colossal rectangles, linked together by curved wings several storeys high, culminating in an enormous central towered pavilion. It became Paul's favourite residence, where he had kicked his heels during those long years when his mother had held him at a distance from power, the capital and herself. At that time people spoke of the Court at Gatchina as opposed to that of the Tsarina at Tsarskoye Selo.

From the outside, the palace resembles a set of barracks, which appealed to Paul. The approach is very discouraging, with its wide flat open space and its severe buildings which spread their haughty façade for hundreds of yards. The interior, in contrast, was sumptuous. Rinaldi had supervised the slightest detail, and Paul had asked his favourite architect Vincenzo Brenna to perfect the decor. When Alexander III arrived there, the *piano nobile* was far too big for him. Each drawing room could hold a regiment and the ceilings were so high that it was impossible to create the intimate atmosphere so sought after at the time. There remained the mezzanine, formerly the servants' living quarters. There, the architects had gone to the other extreme, and the ceilings were so low that the Tsar, who was very tall, could touch them by lifting his arm. His wife, Maria Feodorovna, however, preferred these small rooms to those grandiose and lugubrious grand apartments; their modest proportions reminded her of her native Denmark. Only her second daughter was able to use the upper floor. In fact, her English governess, Mrs Franklyn, refused to bring up her baby in cramped and badly aired conditions, so the nursery was installed in an enormous drawing room, hung with tapestries depicting biblical scenes. Mrs Franklyn resembled a grenadier both in size and by her plain speaking. One day, when a particularly choleric old general was admonishing a sentinel on the palace terrace, Mrs Franklyn opened the window and with a stentorian voice cried out: 'Less noise, general, if you please, less noise.' The old military

---

One of the charming pavilions in Gatchina's impressive park, which was landscaped with lakes, rivers and islands.

IMPERIAL
PALACES OF
RUSSIA

A view of the façade of Gatchina, built by Antonio Rinaldi, Catherine II's favourite architect, for her lover, Grigory Orlov. There is something glacial about the enormous Palace, which has six hundred rooms.

gentleman lifted up his head and stopped in mid-sentence.

There were five thousand employees at Gatchina, for the property consisted not only of the palace and its stables, but also of farms, gardens and factories. All those employed had been carefully chosen, for the most part from families that had served the Romanovs for generations. The members of the family knew them all and called them by their names. 'They were friends,' recalled Mrs Franklyn's pupil, the Grand Duchess Olga.

Alexander III had spartan tastes. He rose at seven o'clock, alone, washed with cold water, dressed himself in peasant's clothes without the help of a valet, made his own coffee in a percolator, filled his plate with biscuits, and having swallowed his breakfast, sat at his desk to begin work for the day. He did not want to disturb anyone, nor did he ring for anyone. Later, the Empress would join him. A small table was brought by two servants, and husband and wife would share a breakfast of bread and butter and boiled eggs.

Alexander III was a giant, with Herculean strength. He would bend a horseshoe or a silver tray as if it were nothing, and tear a pack of cards as if it were a piece of paper. He was a straight and honest man, a conservative with rather straightforward ideas. In contrast to his predecessor, he adored his wife and he adored Gatchina, unlike his entourage who found the house uncomfortable and the life they led there boring in the extreme. Indeed, the sovereigns liked to lead a quiet bourgeois exitence. The Emperor would receive ministers whom he would invite to lunch, as well as high ranking officers, and civil servants who, in contrast, did not have the right to sit at the Imperial table.

At night, they dined intimately. Alexander III would stay for an hour or so talking to his wife and smoking cigarettes, then he would return to his study to work until the small hours. When an official ceremony recalled the Imperial couple to St Petersburg, they would go for the day, borrowing the Imperial train. This consisted of rather old carriages, hung with pink damask, with large quantities of plush, lace and trimmings. The armchairs were nailed to the floor at a respectable distance one from another, and according to a traveller who sat on them frequently, they were unbearably uncomfortable.

In spite of the simplicity which they espoused, the ceremonial way of life never left the members of the Imperial family. Their teachers would teach the Grand Dukes and Grand Duchesses in full dress and wearing their decorations. Even the American dentist who peered into the Imperial children's mouths would pin back his tails and fold back his sleeves, and had a row of imposing medals glittering on his chest.

The family meals took place in a bathroom – not any bathroom, since it had belonged to the Empress Alexandra, the wife of Nicholas I. Alexander III and his wife liked this room which looked onto a rose garden. Maria Feodorovna had filled the enormous bath with azaleas. In spite of the countless marvels which emerged from the Imperial kitchens, the Romanov children were always hungry. Given their age, they were always placed at the bottom of the table, and when they had been served the Emperor and his guests had already finished, so they barely had time to touch what was on their plates before they were whisked away.

They had the most beautiful playroom in the world. It was in the basement,

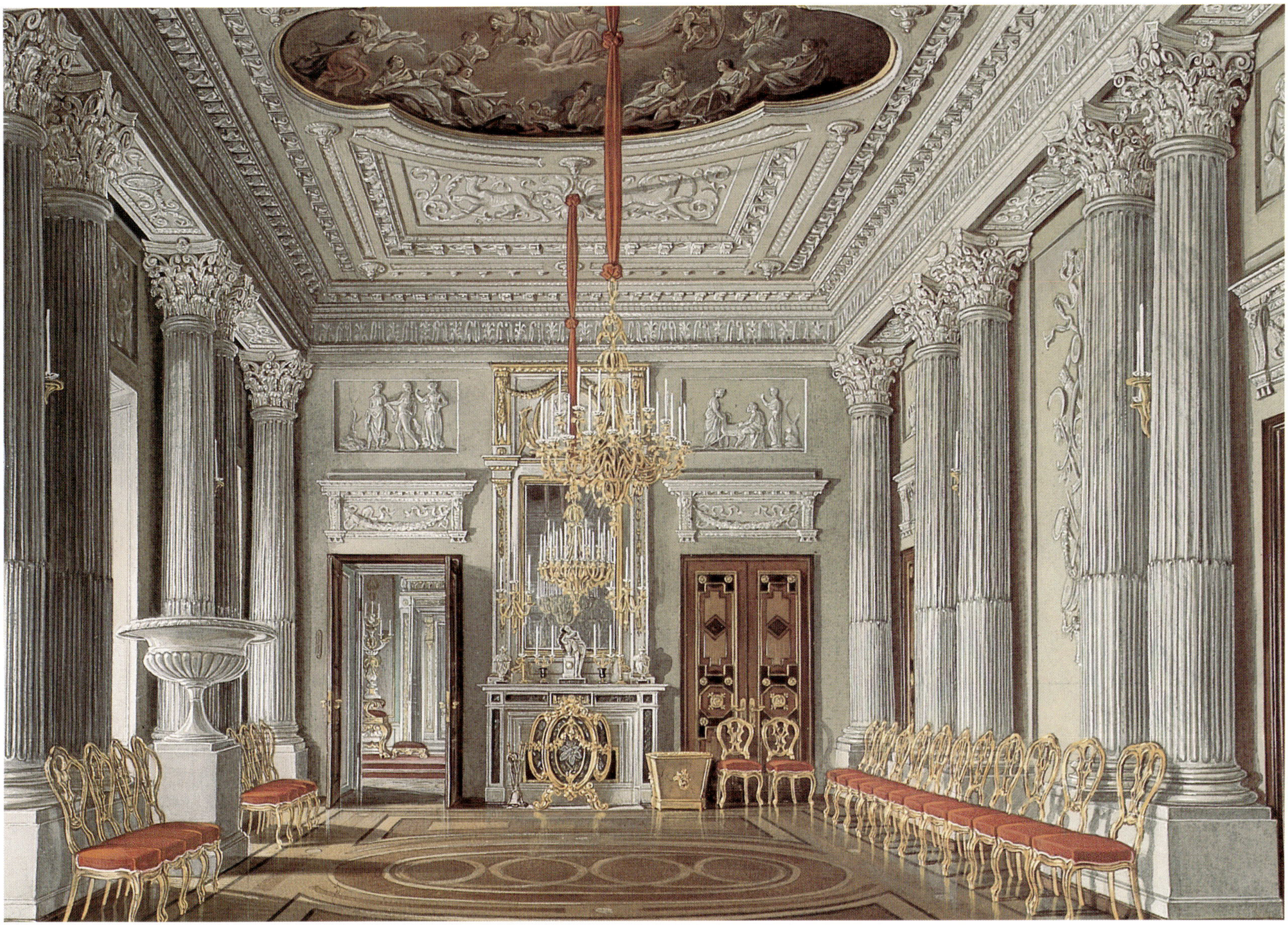

The marble dining room, watercolour by E. G. Hau, 1880. Under Alexander III the Imperial family ate its meals in what had been Empress Alexandra Feodorovna's bathroom. Nevertheless, the room is very charming, with a view over the rose garden.

The white hall, watercolour by E. G. Hau, 1880. After damage inflicted during the Second World War, restoration work has begun at Gatchina. The white hall has been restored to its original beauty when occupied by Prince Orlov.

Far right Empress Alexandra Feodorovna's bedroom, watercolour by E. G. Hau, 1880. The vaulted ceiling adds to the slightly airless feel of this room, where furniture and trinkets crowd in with upholstery and plush.

a room with vaulted ceilings, interspersed with square columns, where toys from all over the world were gathered: dolls' houses unlike any other, but best of all a mechanical train set with yards and yards of track, huge quantities of locomotives, wagons, stations and people, with which the children never tired of playing. But like all the young, they preferred to do mischief and go to places that were forbidden. They played hide-and-seek in the Chinese gallery where priceless porcelains and jades were displayed. It was so amusing to hide behind, or in, a Ming vase. Or they would run along the Chesme gallery, where tapestries and paintings depicting the victory over the Turks were displayed. The only place the children refused to go was Paul I's bedroom, high up in one of the towers, where they had placed the bloody sheets which had been wrapped round his corpse. Everyone knew that it was badly haunted, and the servants would tell the terrified children that they had often seen the ghost of the assassinated Emperor.

Gatchina's glory is its park, the largest and most picturesque of the Imperial parks, an extraordinary symphony of terraces, lakes, rivers and islands crowned with gracious pavilions. Every breed of dog was kept in the nearby kennels, from the gracious borzoi to the colossal bulldog used to hunt bears. In the stables, a

Empress Maria Feodorovna's study, watercolour by E. G. Hau, 1877. Similar decor can be found in all the rooms at Gatchina illustrated by Hau at the end of the nineteenth century. Victorian styles here blend harmoniously with more typical Russian luxuriousness.

Drawing room of Alexander II, watercolour by E. G. Hau, 1874. In contrast to his father, Nicholas I's, austere tastes, Alexander II favoured the rococo style with its plethora of gilt, paintings, objects, small tables and books.

IMPERIAL PALACES OF RUSSIA

The gardens at Gatchina, watercolour by Meier, 1844. The architecture of Gatchina was severe, so the Palace became well known for its gardens – a succession of ponds, lakes and spinneys.

Chesme gallery, watercolour by E. G. Hau, 1877. This gallery, designed for Catherine II, was later used to display large paintings illustrating the Russian victories over the Turks, and is named after the most famous.

The Empress' reception room, watercolour by E. G. Hau, 1874. This is a most unsympathetic reception room, with its heavy furniture and boldly striped wallpaper.

FAR RIGHT Alexander II's study, water by E. G. Hau, 1882. This intimate and masculine room reflects the character of its occupant, with its collection of small family portraits, comfortable armchair and lounging dog.

IMPERIAL PALACES OF RUSSIA

Boudoir, watercolour by E. G. Hau, 1879. In contrasts with the opulence of other rooms in the Palace, this boudoir is surprisingly simple. The green screen, leather upholstered furniture and simple etchings do not evoke the femininity one might expect.

Drawing room of Empress Alexandra Feodorovna, watercolour by E. G. Hau, 1876. This is a formal, yet rather beautiful room of the Palace.

Oak study in the arsenal wing at Gatchina, watercolour by E. G. Hau, 1877. This study is possibly the most remarkable room at Gatchina painted by Hau, with its wallpapers of bands of flowers alternating with bright yellow wood – typical of the period.

GATCHINA PALACE

State bedrooms, late nineteenth-century watercolour by L. Premazzi. The room is reminiscent of the one illustrated at Pavlovsk, with its bed surrounded by a gilded balustrade in imitation of a bedroom at Versailles.

Maria Feodorovna's boudoir, watercolour by E. G. Hau, 1879.

palace in themselves, an army of grooms and trainers looked after hunting horses.

Alexander III liked exercise and the outdoors. He was also an attentive father, revered by his children. Each afternoon, he would drag them outside, most often to the deer park. In the winter, each one had a spade, a lantern and an apple. He would teach them how to dig a path in the snow and how to make a fire. They would then roast the apples and at nightfall return by the light of their lanterns. In the summer, he would teach them to recognize animals' footprints. He gave them rowing lessons, or they would fish in the full waters of Gatchina. My father only had good memories of Gatchina: 'Our greatest joy was to have a picnic on those long summer evenings when darkness does not really fall, and is replaced by a kind of soft grey twilight which slowly fills the sky.' They would travel to their picnic spot in little Russian carriages, with those back-to-back seats in the shape of horsehoes tied together, 'the cook and his satellites taking up the rear'. While the Emperor and Empress would go off to explore the surroundings with their guests, the young members of the family had nothing better to do than to help the cooks, that is to say to get in their way and to spread happy confusion.

Badly damaged during the last war by the Germans, Gatchina was let to government organizations. It is only recently that its restoration has been undertaken. The decor of the official rooms has been minutely reconstituted and has recovered its original bloom. Furniture and paintings have been brought from elsewhere to give it a true atmosphere. It is finally open to the public and the palace has begun to come back to life.

RIGHT Watercolour of the gardens at Gatchina, showing the studied mix of water and foliage. FAR RIGHT View of the Palace from across the vast lake.

Anichkov Palace

AT the point where the Fontanka canal crosses the Nevsky Prospekt, the longest and most popular thoroughfare in St Petersburg, there was an encampment, when the city was first founded, commanded by a certain Colonel Anichkov who gave his name to the palace that was built there. In 1741, Tsarina Elizabeth Petrovna bought the plot in order to build a palace there for her lover Alexei Razumovsky. She chose the Russian architect Mikhail Zemstov (1688–1743), who died two years later, leaving his assistant to complete the task. It was in the rich baroque style, with pavilions topped with golden onion domes and golden statues bearing the Tsarina's monogram. After Razumovsky's death, then that of Elizabeth, Catherine gave the palace to her lover Potomkin, who, perpetually in debt, sold it on to a merchant. Catherine, always obliging, bought it back and gave it once again to Potomkin, who instructed the architect Vasili Stasov to modify it. The palace was altered, with the addition of a third floor on the wings and the replacement of the golden onion domes with classic cupolas. Whereupon, with his customary effrontery, Potomkin, once again in debt, sold the palace back to the Imperial treasury.

At the beginning of the nineteenth century, Alexander I instructed the architect Quarenghi to use the space between the palace and the Fontanka to install a row of shops selling the Imperial factories' products: porcelain, glass, bronze, tapestries and silks. Quarenghi built a very elegant double colonnade surmounted by a balustrade decorated with statues.

Later, Alexander I decided that his offices needed more room, which could be found in the Anichkov Palace, which consequently was once again altered. The shops in Quarenghi's colonnade were closed. The architect Luigi Rusca (1758–1822) enlarged the building by adding two wings, but the Imperial chancellery still needed more space and they had to close a section of the colonnade to create offices. It was now decided that the palace itself would become the residence of the heir to the throne, so more alterations were made by the architect Carlo Rossi, Alexander I's favourite. As was his habit, he did not stop at the external architecture, but decorated the entire interior and even redesigned the surrouding area. He cut off a large part of the garden to create Ostrovsky Square around which he built the Alexandreisky Theatre, now the Pushkin Theatre, and the National Library.

The future Nicholas I lived at Anichkov before his tumultuous accession to the throne, as did the future Alexander III. The latter built a covered hall over which he put a winter garden, which completely altered the eighteenth-century façade. When he was in town, which used to happen in spite of his passion for Gatchina, he refused to live at the Winter Palace, but remained at Anichkov. In

---

A detail of the ceiling decoration in the gold drawing room at Anichkov.

IMPERIAL PALACES OF RUSSIA

spite of his simplicity, Alexander III, conscious of the Empire's standing, knew how to make the grand Court ceremonials an unforgettable spectacle. He was helped in this by his wife, the Empress Maria Feodorovna, who, unlike him, enjoyed society, balls and dancing. Always elegant, gracious and smiling, she entertained marvellously, charming all those who got near her. Although small, no sooner had she entered a room than all heads turned towards her. Nobody could curtsey better than she. Under her rule, the Court became supremely elegant, as recalled by Maria of Rumania, who, as daughter of a Grand Duchess, often stayed at the Court of St Petersburg:

> In the place of honour stand Uncle Sasha and Aunt Mini, in those days Emperor and Empress. Her golden dress is all covered with silver embroidery and she is crowned with a tiara of sapphires so large that they look like enormous eyes. Cascades of pearls and diamonds hang round her throat down to her waist. She is the only one among the royal ladies whose gown is crossed by the blue order of St Andrew, while the the Grand Duchesses wear the red ribbon of St Catherine. Aunt Miechen (Grand Duchess Vladimir) stands close behind. Her gold embroidered orange gown is more gorgeous than the sunset. When she moves, the pearls of her diadem swing gently backwards and forwards. She is not thin enough for classic lines, but she is very close, better than the other women present. Her shoulders are superb and as white as cream. There is a smartness about her that no one else can attain. And there, beside her, stands my mother (the Duchess of Edinburgh), curiously at home in that radiant assembly, much more at home than she is in London or Windsor. Her gown is deep gentian blue trimmed with sable, and the rubies she wears are like enormous drops of blood. Aunt Ella (the Grand Duchess Sergei) is dressed in 'old pink' and silver, and her perfect face is crowned with diamonds like flashing rays of light. Amongst the older ones is Aunt Sani (the Grand Duchess Alexandra Yossifovna), a chip off the old block, who stands like a proud pillar of the past generation. Mother of Olga, Queen of Greece, she is a magnificent presence. Clothed all in silver, as upright as a tree, she is tall and imposing. Age has not bent her shoulders nor lowered her head. The diamonds on her white hair are like hoar frost in the snow, and she wears more pearls than anyone present, which fall in thick cascades over the red ribbon of her order. She is quite aware of what suits her and is indeed a proud old ancestor among those so much younger than her. And what an array of uniforms, how tall are all my uncles and cousins. I am almost afraid to look at them, but how superbly handsome some of them are. There are, I must confess, one or two really ugly old uncles amongst them, but they are outnumbered by the others, and are but shadows heightening their brilliance. I lower my eyes, only to lift them once again to gaze on those who fascinate me, like so many figures in an incredible dream.

Maria of Rumania does not mention in her account the 'fabulous Kochubey', the grand mistress of the Court, Princess Kochubey, a formidable lady, probably the last of her kind, immensely rich, mistress of an accomplished household, unforgiving in matters of protocol. It was whispered that she could recite the Gotha Almanach through from beginning to end. Everyone shook before her and she ruled the Court with a rod of iron.

Alexandra Feodorovna's study, watercolour by L. Premazzi, 1853. In the nineteenth century Anichkov was occupied by the heir to the throne, the future Nicholas I, and his wife. It provided exceptionally sumptuous surroundings, with marble vases, old master paintings and plush, yet rather simple furniture.

Alexandra Feodorova's bedroom, watercolour by E. G. Hau. Again, this is evidently a state, rather than an occupied, bedroom, with its imposing bed surrounded by obelisks and marble vases.

IMPERIAL PALACES OF RUSSIA

Never was Alexander III's Herculean stength more useful than during an accident, or possible assassination attempt, on the Imperial train. On its way to the Crimea, it derailed and the roof of the carriage would certainly have crushed his family if the Tsar had not held it up with the sheer strength of his arms until people came to the rescue. The effort had, however, been too much for him. He suffered a kidney disease and died at the age of forty-nine. Naturally, nothing was ready to receive the new Emperor, Nicholas II.

He continued to live at Anichkov with his mother, who had inherited it. The Court mourning period of six months was lifted only for a single day to allow him to marry his fiancée, Alix of Hesse, whom he had taken much trouble in persuading to give him her hand. As dawn was breaking on that memorable 26 November 1894, the crowd began to fill the square in front of the palace. Every class of society in the Empire had been invited, so a woman with a diamond tiara found herself next to a peasant wearing a caftan, and the gold braided uniform of a Court functionary could be found next to the sombre tunic of a village mayor.

Well before eleven o'clock, the hour fixed for the ceremony, the rooms of the Winter Palace were full to bursting. Everyone was waiting. Minutes passed, then a quarter of an hour, half an hour, three quarters of an hour. Everyone was asking what was happening. In the Anichkov Palace, where the bride was dressing, the over-zealous police had arrested the French hairdresser, the famous Monsieur Decroix, who dressed all the Grand Duchesses' hair on their wedding days, but who had forgotten to bring his invitation. In her room, the future Tsarina waited, becoming more and more anxious as to his whereabouts. Finally, one of the Emperor's valets recognized the poor man and allowed him to enter the palace to begin his work on Alexandra's auburn hair. It was only at midday, an hour late, that the grand master of ceremonies announced the arrival of the procession. Nicholas was wearing the red uniform of his regiment of hussars, with its white and gold jacket negligently thrown over the shoulder, as was the practice. When the guests saw the one who was very soon to become their Tsarina, they all cried out: 'Isn't she beautiful?' Alix was wearing a silver dress which went marvellously with her long veil of old lace. She was wearing the diadem reserved for this occasion, a diamond pyramid with a very big pink diamond at the centre, which had been bought by Paul I. Around her neck and on her bodice she wore more diamonds, which were part of the crown jewels reserved for the wife of the sovereign. Over her shoulders, she had thrown a very long gold brocade coat bordered with ermine.

Behind her came the Dowager Empress on the arm of her father, the old King of Denmark. In spite of her efforts to forget her husband's death, her eyes were red and sadness could be read on her face. Then came Maria Feodorovna's sister, the ravishing Princess of Wales, always exceedingly elegant, with her husband, the future Edward VII. After the wedding breakfast, Niki and Alix left in a Court coach pulled by six white horses. A huge and enthusiastic crowd were waiting for them. Alix was waving mechanically and her eyes were full of tears. Her subjects did not yet know that she was almost clinically shy.

The young couple re-entered Anichkov Palace, where the Dowager was waiting for them, still wearing her Court dress. She led them to their apartments. Maria Feodorovna had decided that since the Imperial apartments at the Winter Palace were not ready, the young couple would continue to live with her. Their residence was minute, consisting of a few rooms on the ground floor which Nicholas II had shared with his brother during their childhood. The Imperial couple did not even have a dining room and had to take their meals with the Dowager who, as mistress of the house, sat at the head of the table. The new Empress only had a tiny drawing room. So the richest masters in the world, owners of countless vast palaces, began their reign in a crowded apartment that would have been rejected by a tradesman.

Colour lithograph showing Anichkov as it was when built in the eighteenth century by the architect Mikhail Zemtsov (1688–1743). Today, with its flattened roofs and Quarenghi's famous colonnade lining the façade, it is almost unrecognizable.

Grand Duke Vladimir's Palace

ICHOLAS II was a timid and impressionable man who always allowed his uncles, the late Alexander III's brothers, to impose on him. They were all very tall, handsome, with powerful personalities, who always spoke their minds and who considered their nephew as a youngster who needed to be corrected occasionally.

Grand Duke Vladimir was the most formidable of the lot, a womanizer and a sensualist, with an indomitable character, who was very cultured and had the discerning taste of a well-informed collector. His palace was situated at the corner of the Winter Quay and the appropriately nicknamed 'Millionaire's Row'. The exterior is surprising, in a kind of Italian style. The inside mixes all manner of styles – the sumptuous marble staircase refers to the baroque, the large drawing room is Renaissance, the small dining room Gothic, the ballroom completely rococo and, finally, the banqueting hall reintroduces the old Russian style.

At the time, people were beginning to tire of looking for inspiration in all the European arts. They began to search into Russia's past, and the themes and forms of Russia in the Middle Ages began to re-emerge. It immediately became a rage that Russian ballet grandiosely illustrated. Grand Duke Vladimir had the insight to follow this tendency at the outset and had his palace decorated with frescos.

He had married Princess Marie of Mecklenburg-Schwerin, 'Aunt Miechen' to Maria of Rumania and the family. She was by far the most elegant wife in the Court. She spent without counting, collecting jewels, but nobody was better suited to wear so many. As Maria of Rumania remarked: 'All through life, she has been cherished, adulated, spoiled… An atmosphere of unlimited prosperity emanated from her. She was the indisputed centre of her world, the very sight of her invited attention…' Intelligent, ambitious, authoritarian, she was charm and courtesy itself, and became the queen of St Petersburg society, as Grand Duchess Helen had been a century earlier. Her salon was the most brilliant in town. Ministers, diplomats, artists and foreigners would gravitate there. She kept open house and all boasted of her incomparable hospitality. If between her and her sister-in-law, the Empress Maria Feodorovna, a prudent neutrality had been established, she clearly provoked antipathy in the new Tsarina, Alexandra Feodorovna.

Grand Duke Vladimir's Florentine-inspired Palace was built in the 1870s. The interiors reflected a plethora of styles: the Turkish smoking room is pictured here. Although oriental in appearance, the room uses marbles which would have been alien to Ottoman architects. It is nevertheless a delicate caprice designed for masculine relaxation.

IMPERIAL PALACES OF RUSSIA

Soon unpleasant family affairs were involved. Maria Pavlovna's son, Cyril, married the Tsarina's brother's divorced wife, something which the Tsarina never forgave. Maria Pavlovna's dislike of Alexandra turned to contempt. She clearly saw the disaster the Empire was heading for well before the Revolution. When it erupted, the Grand Duchess took refuge in the Crimea and this woman on whom life had smiled so much and who had owned everything lived there in the most terrible conditions. She had the luck to be rescued from that hell by her parents. When they saw her again after many years of separation, her children did not recognize her. That imposing and spirited woman had become a haggard skeleton. She only lived a few more months.

GRAND DUKE VLADIMIR'S PALACE

In this sumptuous red and gold drawing room overlooking the Neva, Grand Duke Vladimir's wife, Maria Pavlovna, the Queen of St Petersburg society, received her many distinguished guests.

Belosseilsky Belosievsky

RAND Duke Sergei was by far the best housed of all Alexander III's brothers. In 1884, the Crown purchased for him the splendid palace belonging to Prince Belosievsky, built on the corner of the Fontanka canal, on the other side from the Anichkov Palace. It is Andrei Stakenschneider's masterpiece, the most perfect and seductive rococo pastiche in the world. This marvel looks as if it were built in the eighteenth century, instead of the middle of the nineteenth, well after the period to which it belongs. Sergei had the good taste to keep the original decor almost intact, limiting himself to adding a room here or his monogram there on a staircase.

By all accounts he was a very unappealing man, very good looking, cold, with a dark and bizarre side to him which his contemporaries preferred not to look into too deeply. He had married Elizabeth of Hesse, the Tsarina Alexandra's sister, 'Aunt Ella' for Maria of Romania, a ravishing beauty whom he showered with jewels. When she entertained at the Belosseilsky Belosievsky, she would go upstairs in the middle of the ball to change into a new dress, even more beautiful than the last, and an even richer set of jewels.

Appointed Governor of Moscow, Grand Duke Sergei showed himself to be so hard and so incompetent that he was in large part responsible for the terrible accident which cost the lives of three thousand Moscovites during the coronation of Nicholas II. The nihilists did not fail in their attempt to kill him. In 1905, when he was leaving the Kremlin in a carriage, he was blown up by a bomb. His widow obtained permission to visit his assassin in prison, and she sought without success to have his sentence commuted. This beautiful woman, who had dazzled the world, now retired completely from it. She founded a monastery where she became abbess. During the Revolution, she was arrested and imprisoned at Perm, with several other members of the Imperial family. Together, they were thrown down a mineshaft, into which their assassins threw grenades. When their remains were discovered, it was proved that they had survived for several days, covered in wounds, starving and dying of thirst. The martyred body of the Grand Duchess Elizabeth is today buried in Jerusalem, where it has become an object of veneration.

LEFT In the foreground is one of the four horses which guard the Anichkov Bridge, whilst behind are the windows of the corner drawing room of the Palace.

OVERLEAF The Palace was cleverly designed by the architect Andrei Stakenschneider to create a triumphant pastiche of rococo styles.

IMPERIAL
PALACES OF
RUSSIA

Previous pages This detail above a door in the opulent corner drawing room is characteristic of late nineteenth-century rococo decoration, with its indispensible *putti* and abundant gilding.

Above Belosseilsky Belosievsky Palace, nineteenth-century colour lithograph by J. Charlemagne. The rococo Palace is seen with the famous Anichkov bridge in the foreground. **Below** The full front façade of the Palace as it appears today.

198

ABOVE The fireplace in the corner drawing room demonstrates the excesses of late nineteenth-century rococo style which would never have appeared in the eighteenth century.

LEFT Detail of a door in the red dining room, showing the exquisite colours of painted stucco for which St Petersburg is famous.

Tsarskoye Selo and the Winter Palace under Nicholas II

ICHOLAS II and Empress Alexandra were soon to become obsessed with one idea: to escape from Anichkov Palace. Although there were also problems of security, their most important priority was to protect their intimacy, for from the first day they met right up until their tragic death they were to remain madly in love with each other. Their choice of a new residence fell on the Alexander Palace at Tsarskoye Selo. It was a very large house, rather than a palace, set in an isolated corner of the huge estate. Catherine II had had it built for her favourite grandson, Alexander I. Giacomo Quarenghi had drawn up plans for the new building, creating a masterpiece in the purest neo-classical Palladian style. It has no outer ornamentation, except a double row of columns which links the two isolated pavilions which constitute the palace complex. All the art of the Alexander Palace rests in the nobility of its design and form. The redecoration work at Alexander Palace was quickly finished under pressure from the impatient couple, so much so that a year after the death of Alexander III, Nicholas II could write to his mother:

> When we entered Alix's apartment, we could hardly get over the pleasant surprise we felt when we saw that nothing had been left that could possibly remind us of the dreadful old arrrangements. This changed to utter delight when we settled ourselves into these marvellous rooms. Sometimes we simply sit in silence wherever we happen to be and admire the walls, the fireplace and the furniture . . . The mauve room is delightful. One wonders when it looks better, in the evening or by daylight. The bedroom is gay and cosy. Alix's first room, the Chippendale drawing room, is also attractive, all in pale green. But as not all the furniture is ready yet, it is too early to form a definite opinion about it. The stoves in my study and in the dining room have been altered, and they have hung new curtains there. Twice we went up to the future nursery. Here the rooms are also remarkably airy, light and cosy.

Tsarskoye Selo, Alexander I's study, which is symptomatic of this austere Tsar. The ceiling is low compared to those of the state rooms, and the Emperor of all the Russias chose to work on long tables of white wood simply covered with blue cloth.

For the Imperial couple were expecting their first baby. They were hoping for a boy; it was a girl, soon to be followed by three others.

There was a strange contrast between Alexander Palace and its neighbour, Catherine's Great Palace, which was used for the Court ceremonies. There was enough gold, marble, crystal, velvet and silk there to 'put to shame even the most imaginative Hollywood producers'. There were pavilions, monuments, statues, terraces, guards with gold braid, Court coaches pulled by magnificent horses, Court messengers with plumed hats, ladies-in-waiting in precious furs, cordons of police, Cossacks. Whereas at the Alexander Palace there was all the paraphernalia of an English squire: chintzes, maple wood furniture and brass beds.

Nicholas II and Alix hardly ever went to town. As a result, they did not alter the Winter Palace very much: a family dining room, a library in the most monstrous Anglo-Gothic style, and finally a bedroom whose ceiling is decorated with garlands of flowers designed by the Empress herself. The great Court occasions became more and more infrequent. However, in 1903, there was an unforgettable ball where the entire Court wore seventeenth-century Russian dress. The Emperor came as Alexis I in raspberry, gold and silver brocade, decorated with several Crown jewels specially brought from the Kremlin for the occasion. The Empress appeared as Tsarina Maria, his wife, in gold and saffron brocade, embroidered with emeralds. The Grand Dukes wore the robes of their ancestors' courtiers, and the great families had brought out their old heirloom jewellery. They danced old national dances. Grand Duke Michael, Nicholas II's brother, lost the diamond plume that his mother had lent him. In spite of a frantic search, it was never found.

That was the last Court ball. The shy Alexandra refused to undergo another such ordeal, and then events took over. In 1905, Russia fought a disastrous war against Japan. One day, when Nicholas was in Alexandra's famous mauve boudoir, they brought him a telegram. He read it, turned deathly pale and began to tremble so much that he had to lean against a chair to prevent himself from falling. In a tight voice he announced that the entire Russian fleet had been sunk by the Japanese in the Bay of Tsushima. The Empress burst into tears. The whole palace seemed to go into mourning.

Soon after this, the Epiphany celebration took place at the Winter Palace, when the Tsar traditionally took part in the blessing of the waters. The men, Grand Dukes, the diplomatic corps, generals and ministers would line up on the quay of the Neva. The women, in formal Court dress, attended the ceremony from a balcony. Traditionally, the Peter and Paul fortress would fire guns in salute, using blanks of course. But that year, thanks to internal accomplices, revolutionaries managed to put live ammunition in the canons. A policeman just behind the Emperor was badly wounded; the Admiralty building was also hit. The windows of the Winter Palace flew into a thousand pieces, some of which landed on the Dowager Empress and the Grand Duchesses. Confusion reigned, with soldiers and policemen rushing in all directions, no one knowing whether the Emperor had been hit. Luckily his mother and his wife could see him standing, impassive and still. 'I knew,' he would recount later, ' that somebody was trying to kill me. I simply made the sign of the cross. What else could I do?' He picked up a bit of shrapnel which had fallen next to him and Fabergé

The chapel at Tsarskoye Selo, situated at the extreme north of the Palace façade, with characteristic golden onion domes.

mounted it into a precious object.

This was soon followed by 'Red Sunday', where a demonstration, possibly not that peaceful, degenerated into a terrifying massacre. A revolution shook the entire Empire. The Emperor ordered the Imperial family to leave the capital. The Dowager Empress refused point blank to leave, and her son had to use every imaginable pressure before she finally gave way and retired to Gatchina. As for the Imperial couple, they no longer moved from Tsarskoye Selo. They lived more and more in a closed capsule. Inside it was an enchanted domain, well-managed, spruce, rural, and all around there was violence which one could neither see nor hear. Each day, the Emperor would receive ministers, civil servants and ambassadors. He would sometimes invite them to lunch, but he had no other distraction. The Imperial family was sufficient unto itself.

In spite of his conservatism, Nicholas had to give way to events and accept the formation of a Duma, or assembly, the first step towards a parliamentary system. He returned to the Winter Palace for its inauguration and his niece, Maria Pavlovna (who bore the same name as her aunt), attended along with the rest of the Court.

> The day of the opening of the assembly, the Winter Palace resembled a fortress, so much did they fear an assassination attempt or hostile demonstrations. The Court went out in gala dress, the men in uniforms, the women in dresses with trains and tiaras. I wore a train of the regulation length and took my place in the procession just like a grown-up. There had never been a ceremony like it. Everything was a bit vague and quite a few of the participants did not really know their lines. Most of them had a lugubrious air, and one could easily have thought oneself at a funeral. The Emperor himself, in spite of his ability to hide his feelings, looked sad and nervous.

The revolution then calmed down. Things appeared to return to normal, and the peaceful routine at Tsarskoye Selo was resumed. The young Baroness Buxeveden, who was to become the Empress' favourite lady-in-waiting, was invited to Alexander Palace and was shown into the mauve boudoir. She immediately noticed the deep comfortable armchairs, the unusual collection of paintings crowded on the walls, the piano, the sofa covered in a square of lace, photographs displayed everywhere, and huge bunches of white lilac in big vases spread all around the room. The Empress approached her, wearing one of those fashionable tea gowns of the period in pink silk trimmed with lace. The four little Grand Duchesses, all dressed the same in white with blue ribbons in their hair, greeted her timidly, looking at her as if she were a strange animal. Isa Buxeveden succeeded in relaxing and taming them and soon the little girls were playing animatedly with her. Suddenly, the Empress ordered everyone to be silent. They were bringing the baby, the Grand Duke Alexis, heir to the throne, the long-awaited son, the apple of the Empress' eye. Isa saw the most beautiful baby, with very big dark blue eyes. He was somewhat plump and had very pink cheeks which dimpled when he smiled. He held his arms out to his mother who, as soon as she laid eyes on her child, radiated happiness. She so liked Isa that she handed the baby for her to hold for a few moments. As everyone knows, this seductive child was his mother's constant torture, for he had been born with

View through the doorways of successive rooms at Tsarskoye Selo, which creates an impression typical of Russian palaces: suites of rooms lead on one from the other, each more richly decorated than the last.

haemophilia, that incurable illness which threatened his life at every moment.

At eight o'clock in the evening, Isa rejoined the Imperial family for dinner. Nicholas and Alexandra did not have a dining room. The meals were served in whichever room they happened to choose at the last moment. That evening, it took place in the Empress' little yellow drawing room. In the antechamber, Isa saw the cooks in their white hats, the illustrious Mr Kubatat their head, who stood among the plates with silver covers, tasting the dishes here and there. The Empress had changed; she was wearing blue and silver, with countless rows of pearls around her neck and a sort of little cape embroidered with pearls on her head. Isa fell under the Emperor's charm. Each time he smiled, his grey eyes would crease up. He was a gentle, affable man, always attentive and considerate, a born charmer.

After dinner, they returned to the Empress' boudoir. Nicholas took his tea in a gold-mounted glass with a handle. He dived into a pile of white envelopes, where an orange silk thread had been passed under each seal to assist their opening. They contained dispatches and reports. Sometimes, while he was reading, he would pass a piece of paper to the Empress, without either of them making a comment. Alexandra had stretched herself out on her *chaise-longue*, with its lace-covered cushions. Behind her stood a glass screen which protected her from draughts, and over her legs she had thrown a lace shawl lined with mauve muslin. The Emperor lit a cigarette which he pushed into his cigarette holder shaped like a little pipe. He began to talk to his aide-de-camp and the duty lady-in-waiting, then he kissed the children, said goodbye to his wife and returned to his study to work.

Once again this idyllic peace, this perfectly harmonious family life, was interrupted by events. In the summer of 1914, the First World War was approaching. The young Grand Duchess Maria Pavlovna was present on the day of its declaration:

> On 2 August I went with Dimitri (her brother) in an open victoria to the Winter Palace, where the Emperor was about to declare war... There was such a crowd on the square in front of the Winter Palace that we had trouble passing, and had to advance at walking pace, stopping all the time. The huge crowd was quiet, their faces solemn and bright. The flags flapped in the air above our heads and the church banners shone in the sun. It seemed that for the first time the people had realized the seriousness of the situation. The Te Deum sung in the Nicholas Hall brought together the Imperial family, the Court and the authorities. After the service and the reading of the declaration, the Emperor and Empress went out onto the balcony. The crowd then fell on their knees and the Russian national hymn, harmonious and impressive, rang out from a thousand breasts.

The war gave the Empress another pretext for leading the retiring life she so enjoyed. She would take her daughters to the military hospitals erected around the palace and would tend to the wounded. The Emperor would often go to the front, taking the heir to the throne with him. After the initial victories, the situation took a turn for the worse, and the enemy's armies began to invade the Empire. The favourite, whom the whole of Russia spoke of with horror, the

A view through one of two archways leading into the courtyard of Alexander Palace, Tsarskoye Selo.

IMPERIAL PALACES OF RUSSIA

RIGHT A detail of the colonnade of Alexander Palace, Tsarskoye Selo. For several years after the Revolution the decor of the Palace was kept intact, but it was badly damaged in the Second World War, and subsequently allowed to deteriorate.

Striking view of the full front façade of Tsarskoye Selo Palace.

OVERLEAF The Egyptian Gate at Tsarskoye Selo. The Palace was adapted to the tastes of the successive Tsars who occupied it. After Napoleon Bonaparte's Egyptian campaign, styles borrowed from the Egyptian architecture became popular, and in the nineteenth century one of the portals in the large gardens was covered with bas-reliefs of pharoahs and hieroglyphics.

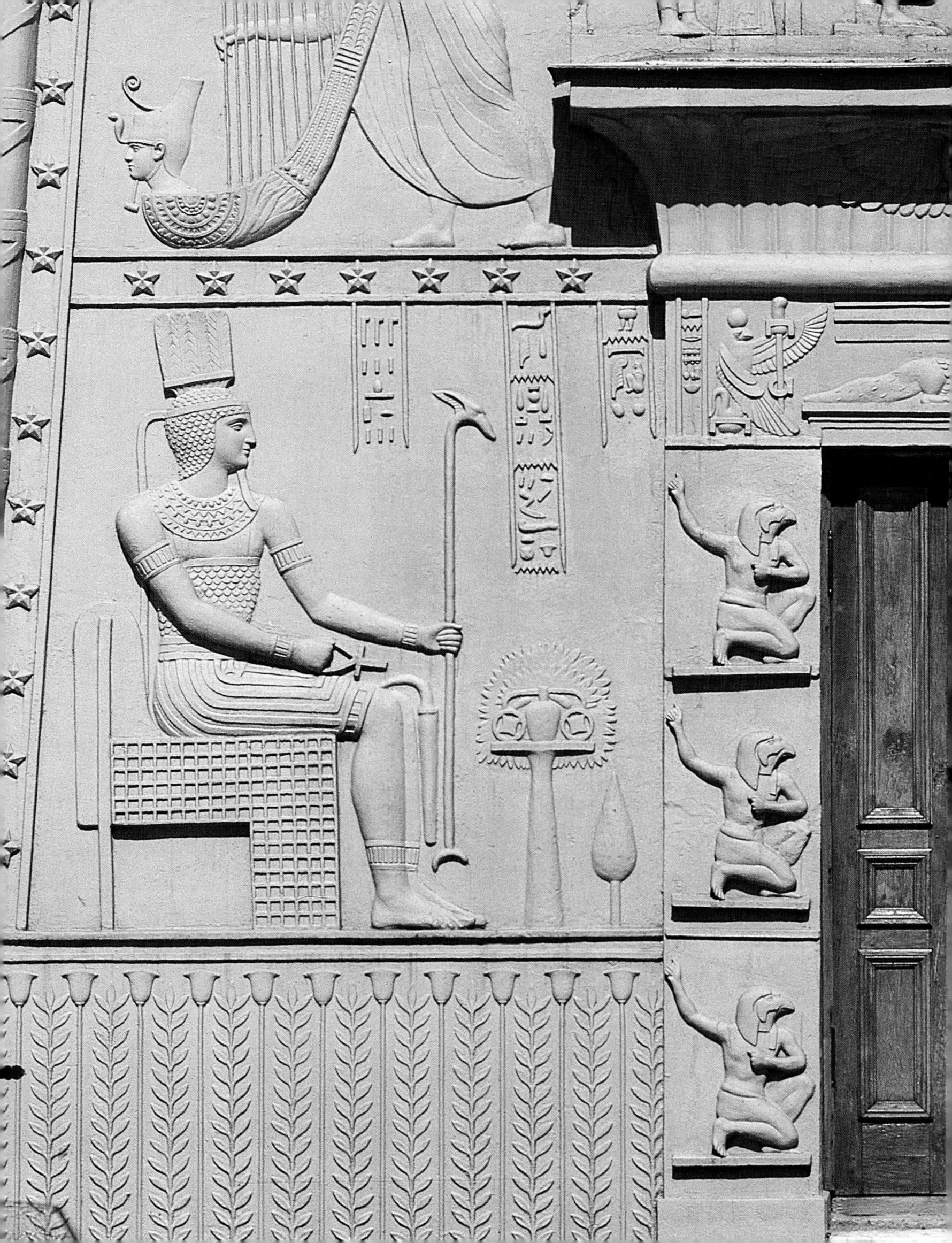

IMPERIAL
PALACES OF
RUSSIA

Tsarskoye Selo and the Winter Palace under Nicholas II

Overall view of Alexander Palace, Tsarskoye Selo, considered to be a masterpiece of its architect, Giacomo Quarenghi.

villainous monk Grigory Rasputin, very debauched but also a great mystic and a disconcertingly accurate prophet, was assassinated. The Empress, beside herself with despair, had him buried at night in a church which she had had built not far from Alexander Palace.

New Year's Day 1917 arrived. As was the custom, the Emperor received the festive greetings in Catherine's Great Palace. It was minus 38 degrees centigrade. The Court coach horses had an armour of ice, and the windows of the coaches were opaque with frost. Nicholas II, impassive, smiling and courteous, greeted each delegation and diplomat in turn, exchanging a banality and affecting an easy manner. However, the heart of the French ambassador, Maurice Paleologue, was heavy:

> Taking us back to the Imperial station, our coaches passed in front of a pretty little isolated church in the Moscovite style. It is the Feodorovsky Sobor, which houses on its lower floor, in a mysterious crypt, Alexandra Feodorovna's favourite chapel. It is already dark. Under its thick shroud of snow, the cupola's outline is barely distinguishable through the mist. I reflect on the hours of sighing exultations or grief-stricken prostrations that the Empress has performed there, and I think I see Rasputin's ghost roaming around the churchyard.

Nicholas set off again for the front and soon the troubles burst out in the capital, now renamed Petrograd. Alexandra, isolated at Tsarskoye Selo, learned that the whole city had fallen into the hands of the Revolutionaries, and that a provisional government had been installed. It was proposed that she be evacuated to Gatchina, further away and more protected, but the children had mumps and could not be moved. In fact, the railways were soon in the hands of the Revolutionaries. On the evening of 13 March 1917, the garrison at Tsarskoye Selo mutinied, shots were fired in the streets and the Revolutionary soldiers approached the palace. They killed a sentry less than five hundred yards from the Empress' residence, then suddenly all the excitement died down. The night passed away in a temporary calm. The next day, the Empress remained cut off from everything, with no news from the capital or from her husband. The third day was as tortured. She became almost mad in this silence and inactivity, with her children ill, without her husband, nor anyone around to advise or inform her.

On 16 March, her uncle by marriage, Grand Duke Paul, came to the house. He found her wearing a nurse's uniform, calm and apparently serene: 'Dear Alix, I wanted to be near you in these difficult times.' Her eyes went straight through him: 'Niki?' Her first thought had been for her husband. 'Niki is well, but be brave, as brave as he has been. Today, at one o'clock in the morning, he signed his abdication and that of Alexis.' She lowered her head as if in prayer. 'If Niki has done that, it was because he had to. I have faith in divine mercy. God will not abandon us.' Big tears began to fall down her cheeks: 'I am no longer Empress,' she said with a sad smile, 'But I remain a sister of charity.' A few days later, she and the children were arrested. The next day, Nicholas II could at last return to Tsarskoye Selo. The reunion between man and wife was moving, painful and wonderful.

In some ways, the Emperor adjusted to his captivity. With his children, he would go into the garden, cut wood and he even created a kitchen garden. Sometimes the guards would be sympathetic to their prisoners, and at others they were unpleasant and insulting, and humiliated them. Nicholas remained smiling and impassive. The Empress was by far the worst affected: her nerves were gone and she never left her *chaise-longue*. Finally, at the beginning of August, it was announced that they were to be transferred to a secret destination. They had orders to be ready by midnight. Towards one o'clock in the morning, they were gathered together with their small quantity of luggage in the semi-circular hall, but the train which was to have taken them had still not arrived: the railwaymen of Petrograd had tried to stop it. Hours passed in uncertainty, weariness and worry. Finally, towards five o'clock in the morning, it was announced that everything was ready. They said goodbye to the palace servants and took their places in the Court cars, whose doors still bore the double-headed eagle. A cavalry detachment escorted them to the little station in the town. They climbed into very comfortable carriages. It was six in the morning when the train left. While the last Tsar of all the Russias was carried away with his family towards their tragic destiny, behind them the Alexander Palace stood empty, silent and dark.

INDEX

Figures in italics refer to captions

Academy of Art 64, 68
Aivasovsky, Ivan 28
Alexander I (formerly Grand Duke Alexander) 68, 82, 84, 89, 113, 131
 Alexander Palace 201, *201*
 Anichkov Palace 183
 assassination of father 116-17, 124
 character 123-4
 death 124, 144
 invasion of Russia 119-20
 Kamennostrovsky Palace 118-20
 Michael's Palace 127
 Winter Palace *40*, 143
 Yelagin Palace 123, *125*
Alexander II 151
 assassination 151, 153, 154, 162, 169
 Gatchina Palace *174*, *176*
 Peterhof *31*
Alexander III 8, 151, 154, 162, 189, 193, 201
 Anichkov Palace 183-4, 186
 art collection 128
 character 180, 186
 Gatchina Palace 169, 172, 180
Alexander Palace 201-2, 206, *206*, *208*, *213*, 214-15
 Feodorovsky Sobor chapel 214
 Mauve boudoir 202, 204, 206
 Yellow drawing room *206*
Alexander Theatre 123
Alexandra Feodorovna, Empress (wife of Nicholas I)
 Anichkov Palace *185*
 Gatchina Palace 172, *173*, 174, *178*
 military uprising 144, 147-8
 Peterhof Cottage 131, 134-5, *136*, 138
 Winter Palace 144, 148, 150-1
Alexandra Feodorovna, Empress (wife of Nicholas II) 189-90, 193
 Alexander Palace 201-2, 204, 206, 214
 Anichkov Palace 186-7, 201
 Revolution 202, 204, 214-15
 Tsarskoye Selo 204, 214-15
 wedding 186-7
 Winter Palace 202, 204
Alexandra of Greece 8
Alexandra of Saxe-Alterburg, Princess 154-5
Alexandra Yossifovna, Grand Duchess 184
Alexandreisky Theatre 183
Alexis I 202
Alexis, Grand Duke 204, 206, 214
Alix of Hesse *see* Alexandra Feodorovna, Empress (wife of Nicholas II)
Anichkov, Colonel 183
Anichkov Bridge *193*, *198*
Anichkov Palace 151, 183-7, *183*, *187*, 193, 201
 Alexandra Feodorovna's bedroom *185*
 Alexandra Feodorovna's study *185*
 Gold drawing room *183*
 Quarenghi's colonnade 183, *187*
Anna Pavlovna, Queen (Holland) 144
Anne (daughter of Peter I) 19, 39, 40
Aparkamakov 114

Balachev, General 119
Barozzi Brothers 53
Bazenov, Vasili 112, *114*, 118, 143
Belosievsky, Prince 193
Belosseilsky Belosievsky Palace 193, *193-9*
Beningsen, Count 114, 116, 118
Benois, Nicholai *29*
Borodino, Battle of 120
Braunstein, I.F. *21*, 23, *23*, *73*
Brenna, Vincenzo 90, *90*, 112, *114*, 123, 169
Brown, Capability 102
Bryullov, Alexander 144
Bush, Joseph 80, 123
Buxeveden, Baroness Isa 204, 206

Cameron, Charles
 Pavlovsk Palace 89, 90, *90*, *92*, 93, 102, *110*
 Tsarskoye Selo *73*, 76, 86, 90
Canova, Antonio *92*
Catherine I, Empress (2nd wife of Peter I) 15, 19, 26, 73
Catherine II (Catherine the Great) 8, 45, 110, 114
 abdication and assassination of Peter III 9, 54-6, 58
 Alexander Palace 201
 Anichkov Palace 183
 art collections 7
 Chesme 64
  death 87
 Gatchina Palace 169, *176*
 Kamennostrovsky Palace 118
 Marble Palace 61, *63*
 Oranienbaum 47-8, *50*, 53-6, *55*
 Pavlovsk Palace 89, *93*
 Peterhof *36*
 relationship with son 89, 112
 Ropcha 58
 Tauride Palace 67-8, *68*, 71
 Tsarskoye Selo 73, *73*, 76, 82, 84, 86-7, *86*, 90
 Winter Palace 82
Catherine Dolgoruky, Princess *see* Yurievskaya, Princess
Catherine, Grand Duchess 119
Charlemagne, J. *63*, *113*, *128*, *198*
Charles XII, King (Sweden) 11, 21
Charlotte of Prussia, Princess *see* Alexandra Feodorovna, Empress (wife of Nicholas I)
Cheremetiev, Count 166
Chertkov 84
Chesme 64, *65*
Chevakinsky, Savva 73, *79*
Choglokov, Mrs 48
Christopher of Greece 8
Circassia, Prince of 22
Clausen, Nicholas *148*
Communism 8, 9-10
 see also Revolution
Constantin, Grand Duke (grandson of Catherine II) 61, 68, 82, 84, 113, 144, 154
Constantine Constantinovich, Grand Duke *63*, 155
Corodini, Giuseppe *79*
Crimean War 162
Custine, Marquis of 131, 134-5, 138
Cyril (son of Grand Duchess Maria Pavlovna) 190

Danilov, General 153
Dawe, George 143
Decroix, Monsieur 186
Demuth-Malinovsky, Vasili *94*, *124*
Denmark, King of 186
Dietz 86
Dimitri (nephew of Nicholas II) 206
Dinglinger, Johann 14
Dolci, Carlo *94*
Duma 71, 204

Edinburgh, Duchess of 184
Edward VII, King (Britain) 186
Elena Vladimirovna, Grand Duchess 8
Elizabeth of Baden 84, 86, 119
Elizabeth of Hesse *see* Ella, Aunt
Elizabeth Petrovna, Tsarina (daughter of Peter I) 19, 45, 54, 68
 Anichkov Palace 183
 Oranienbaum 47
 Peterhof Palace 26
 Summer Palace 112
 Tsarskoye Selo 73, 76, 80
 Winter Palace 39-42
Ella, Aunt (Elizabeth of Hesse, Grand Duchess Sergei) 9, 184, 193
Engineering School 117
Eugene, Viceroy of Italy *see* Leuchtenberg, Duke of

Fabergé 7, 202
Falconet, Étienne-Maurice 76, 147
Fontana, Carlo 47, *50*
Fontanka Canal 183, 193
Fontanka, River 13
Fortress of St Peter and St Paul 11, 13, 42, 166, 202
Franklyn, Mrs 169, 172
Frederic II, Emperor (Prussia) 54
Frederic William I, King (Prussia) 73

Gagarin, Prince 157
Gagarin, Princess 113-14
Gatchina Palace 87, 90, 112, 169-81, *170*, 180, 183, 204, 214
 Alexander II's drawing room *174*
 Alexander II's study *176*
 Alexandra Feodorovna's bedroom *174*
 Alexandra Feodorovna's drawing room *178*
 Bathroom 172, *173*
 Boudoir *178*
 Chesme Gallery 174, *176*
 Chinese Gallery 174
 Empress' reception room *176*
 Kennels and stables 174
 Marble dining room *173*
 Maria Feodorovna's boudoir *179*
 Maria Feodorovna's study *174*
 Oak study *178*
 Park and gardens *169*, 174, *176*, *180*
 Paul I's bedroom 174
 Playroom 172, 174
  restoration 9, *173*, 180
 State bedrooms *179*
 war damage 180
 White Hall *173*
George I, King (Greece) 8
Golovin, Countess 82, 84, 86
Gorky, Maksim 166
Gottardo Gonzago, Pietro di *90*
Gould 102
Goutière 90
Grand Duke Nicholas' Palace 162-5, *162*, *165*
Grand Duke Vladimir's Palace 189-90, *189*, *190*

Hampton Court *29*
Hau, E.G. *31*, 35, *136*, 173, *174*, *176*, *178*, *179*, *185*
Helen, Grand Duchess 189
Helen of Württemberg 127

Imperial Council 157
Imperial Court 7-8
Institute of Smolny 151
Ivan IV 39, 40
Ivan VI 64
Izmailov 56
Izmailovsky Regiment 54

Josephine, Empress 157

Kamennostrovsky Palace 118-21, *119*, *121*
 Gardens 118, *121*
 Oval Hall 118
Katya *see* Yurievskaya, Princess
The King of Judea 155
Klenze, Leo von *144*
Knights of the Order of Malta 90, *106*
Kochubey, Princess 184
Kozlovsky, Mikhail 127
Kronshtadt Island 21, 55
Kutuzov, Field Marshall 119-20

La Chetardière, Ambassador 39
Lamberti (gardener) 53
Le Blond, Alexandre
 Peterhof *22*, 23, *23*, 26, *26*
 Strelna Castle 154
 Summer Garden 19
Le Nôtre, André 23
Lenin, V.I. 166
Lenin Museum 9, 61
Leningrad *see* St Petersburg
Lestocq, Dr 39
Leuchtenberg, Duke of 138, *141*, 157
Louis XIV, King (France) *21*, 26
Louise of Prussia 148

Madame X 131, 134, 138
Mainsky Square 157
Marble Palace 9, 61-3, *61*, *63*
 Marble Hall 61, *61*
Maria Alexandrovna, Princess of Hesse 151
Maria Feodorovna, Empress (wife of Paul I) 110, 119, 124, 147
 Gatchina Palace *174*
 Monument to parents *89*, *110*
 Old Michael's Castle 112, 113, 116
 Pavlovsk Palace 89-90, *94*, *96*, 102, *102*, *106*, 112
 Yelagin Palace 123
Maria Feodorovna (wife of Alexander III, later Dowager Empress) 169, 172, 184, 186-7, 189, *202*, 204
Maria Nikolayevna, Duchess of Leuchtenberg 157, *158*
Maria of Romania 184, 189, 193
Maria Pavlovna, Grand Duchess Vladimir *see* Miechen, Aunt
Maria Pavlovna, Grand Duchess (niece of Nicholas II) 204, 206
Maria, Tsarina (wife of Alexis I) 202
Marie Antoinette, Queen (France) 89
Marie of Mecklenburg-Schwerin, Princess *see* Aunt Miechen
Marinsky Palace 157-60
 Chapel 157, *158*
 Red drawing room 157, *157*
 Rotunda 157, *158*
Marly Palace *21*, *26*
Meier *176*
Menchikov, Prince 15, 19, 47, *50*
Menelaws, Adam 131
Metsu, Gabriel *102*
Meyer, J. *134*
Michael (son of Michael Nicholayevich) 166
Michael, Grand Duke (brother of Alexander I) 127, 202
Michael Nicholayevich, Grand Duke (4th son of Nicholas I) 166, *166*
Michael's Palace 127-9, *128*
 Façade *128*
 Staircase *127*
 White Room 127, *128*
Michetti, Nicolò 21, *21*, *23*, 26
Miconi, Nicoló *148*
Miechen, Aunt (Maria Pavlovna, Grand Duchess Vladimir) 184, 189- 90, *191*
Millionaire's Row 189
Monbijou Palace 73
Monighetti, Ippolito *76*
Montferrand, Auguste Richard de 143
Moscow 7, 120, 193
Moscow Regiment 147
München, Marshall 39, 40

Napoleon Bonaparte *40*, 90, *106*, 113, 117, 124, 157, *208*
 invasion of Russia 118-20, 123
Natichkin, Leon 87
National Library 183
Neielov, Ilya *81*
Neva, River 11, 13, 42, *42*, 61, *63*, 64, 118, *119*, 123, *125*, *166*, *191*, 202
Nevk, River 118
New Michael's Palace 166, *166*
Nicholas I *29*, 127, 131
 Anichkov Palace 183, *185*
 art collection 7
 Gatchina Palace *174*
 Marinsky Palace 157, *158*
 military uprising 144, 147-8
 Peterhof Cottage *7*, *131*, *134*, 138
 Winter Palace 143-4, *144*, 147-8, 150-1
Nicholas II 71, 151
 abdication 214-15
 Alexander Palace 201-2, 206
 Anichkov Palace 186-7, 201
 character 189, 206
 coronation 193
 Revolution 202, 204, 214-15
 Russian Museum 128
 Tsarskoye Selo 204, 214-15
 wedding 186
 Winter Palace 202, 204
Nicholas (son of Michael Nicholayevich) 166
Nicholas Alexandrovich, Grand Duke (son of Alexander II) 151
Nicholas Nikolayevich, Grand Duke (3rd son of Nicholas I) 138, *138*, 162, *162*
Nicholas of Greece 8

Old Michael's Castle 112-17, 118
 Church 112, *114*
 Courtyard 112
 Façade *113*, 114
 Gardens *116*
Olga, Grand Duchess (daughter of Nicholas I) *29*
Olga, Grand Duchess (daughter of Alexander III) 172
Olga, Queen (Greece) (formerly Grand Duchess Olga Constantinovna) 88, 155, 184
Olga Feodorovna, Grand Duchess 166
Oranienbaum 47-56, 143
 Façade *50*
 Chinese Pavilion *48*, *50*, 53, *55*, 58
 Katalnayagorka Pavilion *52*, 54
 Park and gardens 53, *56*
 Peter III's Pavilion 47, *50*
 restoration 9
 Skating Pavilion *5*, *52*
Oranienbaum Canal 47, 53
Orlov, Alexei 54, 58, 64
Orlov, Grigory 54, 56, 58, 61, *63*, 64, 90, 169, *173*
Osterman, Minister 39, 40
Ostrovsky Square 183

Pahlen, Count 114, 116
Palace of Grand Duke Nicholas 138, *138*
Palace of the Duke of Leuchtenberg *141*
Paleologue, Maurice 214
Paul I (formerly Grand Duke Paul) 84, 87, 89, 123, 186
 appearance and character 110-11, 113
 assassination 114-17, 174
 Gatchina Palace 169
 Kamennostrovsky Palace 118
 Mausoleum *106*
 Old Michael's Castle 112-17, *113*, *114*, *116*
 Pavlovsk Palace 90, *94*, 102, *102*, 106, 111
 Tauride Palace 71
Paul, Grand Duke (uncle to Nicholas II) 8, 214
Pavlovsk Palace 8, 89-111, *90*, 112, 154
 Apollo Pavilion *102*
 Apollo's Colonnade *92*, 102
 Aviary *110*
 Bedrooms *179*
 Centaur Bridge *102*
  Courtyard 90, *93*
 'Crick' annd 'Crack' 89
 Drawing Room *108*
 Egyptian entrance hall 90
 Façade *109*
 Friendship Pavilion *111*
 Greek Hall 90, *96*, *106*
 Hall of Peace 90, *96*
 Hall of War 90, *96*
 Italian Hall 90, *106*, *108*
 Knights' room 90, *106*
 Lantern drawing room *94*
 Library *102*
 Maria Feodorovna's state bedroom *102*
 Maria Feodorovna's boudoir *96*
 Maria's Valley 89
 Mausoleum to Paul I *106*
 Monument to parents of Maria Feodorovna *89*, *110*
 Park and gardens 89, *89*, *90*, *92*, *93*, 102, *102*, *109*, 111
 Paul I's study *94*
 Paul's Joy 89
 Picture Gallery *102*
 restoration 90
 Temple of Friendship *93*
 Throne Room *102*
 war damage 9, 90
Pavlovsky Regiment 112
Peobrazensky Regiment 147
Peter I, Tsar (Peter the Great) 40, 73
 assassination attempt 13-14
 dwarf collection 15
 founding of St Petersburg 11, 39
 Peterhof 21-3, *21*, 26, 47, 131
 second marriage 15, 19
 statue 76, 147
 Strelna Castle 154
 Summer Palace *11*, 13-15, *16*, 19, *19*
 Winter Palace 39, *148*
Peter III (formerly Grand Duke Peter) 45, 110, 138
 abdication and assassination 9, 54-6, 58, 64
 art collection 47
 Oranienbaum 47-8, 53-6
 Peterhof 54, 56
Peterhof 21-37, 47, 54, 73, 131, 138, *141*, 143, 154, 155, 169
 Belvedere Pavilion 151
 Farmhouse *31*, *35*
 Fountains *28*
 Great Palace 23, *23*, 26, *26*, *27*, *28*, *32*, *36*
 Hermitage Pavilion *22*, 23
 Island of Olga 29
 Marly Pavilion *21*, 23, 26, *34*
 Mon Plaisir 21, *23*, 26, *34*
 Orangerie *35*
 Park and gardens 23, *29*
 restoration 26, *28*, *32*
 Stables *29*
 war damage 9
Peterhof Cottage 131-41, *131*, *134*, *135*
 Drawing rooms *136*
 Large study *132*, *136*
 Nicholas I's study *7*, *138*
 Staircase *132*
Petrograd *see* St Petersburg
Pimenov, Stephen *124*, 127
Poltava 127
Poniatowski, Stanislaus 61
Potomkin, Grigory 67-8, *68*, 71, 102, 113, 183
Premazzi, L. *179*, *185*
Preobrzhensky Barracks 39
Pretorian Guard of the Streltsy 11
Pugachov 64
Pushkin, A.S. *13*, 117
Pushkin Theatre 183

Quarenghi, Giacomo 7
 Alexander Palace 201, *213*
 Anichkov Palace 183, *187*
 Pavlovsk Palace 90
 Tsarskoye Selo 76, 82, *86*
 Winter Palace 143

Rasputin, Grigory 214
Rastrelli, Bartolommeo 7
 Peterhof *22*, *26*, *26*, *27*
 Summer Palace 112
 Tsarskoye Selo 73, 76, *79*
 Winter Palace *39*, 41, *42*, 143
Razumovsky, Alexis 39, 42, 183
Red Sunday 204
Reni, Guido *94*
Repnina, Princess 48
Repnine, Prince 47
Revolution 10, 61, 157, 166, 190, 202, 204, *208*, 214-15
Ribera, José de *94*
Rinaldi, Antonio 7
 Gatchina Palace 169, *170*
 Marble Palace 61, *63*
 Oranienbaum 47, *50*, 52, 53
Romanov dynasty 7, 172
Ropcha Palace 58, *59*
 Gardens 58
 restoration 9
Rosa, Salvator 155
Rossi, Carlo 7
 Anichkov Palace 183
 Michael's Palace 127, *128*
 Pavlovsk Palace 90
 Yelagin Palace 123, *125*, 127
Rostopchin, Count 120
Rubens, Peter Paul *102*
Rusca, Luigi 183
Russian Museum 128
Russo-Turkish War (1828-29) *76*,
Russo-Turkish War (1877) 162

St Isaac's Cathedral 112, 157
St Michael 112, *116*
St Petersburg (formerly Leningrad and Petrograd) 7, 13, 39, 41, 67, 118, 123, 162, 183, *199*
 Court 127, 184, 189
 flood defences 64
 fortresses 11, 13, 21, 42, 166, 202
 founding of 11
 municipal council 157
 Revolution 214-15
Schaedel, Gottfried 47
Schultz, C. *48*
Sergei, Grand Duchess *see* Ella, Aunt
Sergei Michailovich, Grand Duke 9, 166, 193
Sevigne, Madame de 53
Shislova, Ekaterina 162
Slavyanka, River 89
Smolny Convent 68
Sophie (Regent to Peter I) 11
Stakenschneider, Andrei 7, 138, *141*
 Belosseilsky Belosievsky 193, *193*
 Grand Duke Nicholas' Palace 162, *162*
 Marinsky Palace 157, *158*
 New Michael's Palace 166, *166*
 Winter Palace *45*, 143, 144
Stasov, Vasili 68, *68*, *73*, 143, *147*, 183
Strelna Castle 154-5, *154*
Strogonov, Count 157
Summer Garden *13*, 16, 19, 112, *116*, 151
Summer Palace 13-19, 39, 112
 Admiralty Armchair 13
 Canal façade *19*
 Dining-room 14-15
 Entrance *11*
 Kitchen 14, *16*
 Peter I's bedrooom *16*
 Peter I's study *19*
 Peter I's workshop 14

Talitsin Palace 114
Tatetsvil, Prince 116
Tauride Palace 67-71, 113
 Façade 68, *68*
 Park and gardens 68, 71, *71*
 Rotunda *67*, *71*
Terborch, Gerard *102*
Theatre Marie 143
Thomas of Thomon 118
Tiepolo, Giambattista 53
Torelli, Stefano 53
Trezzini, Domenico 13, 39
Triscorni, Antonio *92*
Tsarskoye Selo Palace 64, 73-87, 90, 123, 143, 150, 169, 204, *204*, 214
 Agate Pavilion 80
 Amber Chamber 73
 Cameron Gallery 80
 Catherine II's apartments 76, 80
 Cave 73
 Church 73, *202*
 Concert Hall *82*, *86*
 Creaking (Chinese) Pavilion 80, *81*
 Egyptian Gate *208*
 English Park 80
 Façade 73, *79*, *208*
 Front courtyard and gates *79*
 Gallery and staircase *73*, 86
 Great Hall 73
 Hermitage 73
 High Bath Pool *84*
 Marble Bridge *76*, *81*
 Monbijou 73
 Turkish Bath *76*, *81*
 Vittolovsky Canal 80, *81*
 war damage 9, 73
 White Pavilion *82*
 see also Alexander Palace; Winter Palace

Union of Soviet Socialist Republics 8-9

Velten, Yuri 19, 64, *65*, 82, 118
Veronese, Paolo *102*
Versailles *179*
Vighi, Antonio *123*, 127, *128*
Vladimir, Grand Duke 189-90, *189*, *190*
Voltaire 53, 58
Voronikhin, Andrei 90, *94*, *102*
Voronstova, Elizabeth 54

Wales, Princess of 186
Wilton House *76*
Winter Quay 166, 189
Winter Palace 39-45, 61, 64, 113, 116, 143-53, *153*, 166, 183, 186, 201-15
 Alexander's Column *40*, 41, 148
 Alexandra Feodorovna's boudoir 144
 balls 148, 150-1, 202
 Chapel 42, 143
 Concert Hall 150
 Diamond Room 144
 Façade *39*, 40
 Hermitage *45*, 143, 148
 Jordan staircase 42, *42*, 143, *143*, 148
 Malachite Rooms 144, *147*, 150
 Military Gallery 143
 New Hermitage *144*
 Nicholas Hall 206
 Nicholas I's study 144
 Nicholas II and Alexandra's family rooms 202
 Pavilion Hall *45*, 143
 rebuildings 39-42, 143
 St George's Hall 143
 Throne Room 143, *148*
 war damage 9
World War I 9, 206
World War II 9, 73, 90, 155, 162, *173*, *208*
Wouwerman, Philip 155

Xenia Alexandrovna, Grand Duchess 58

Yelagin Island 123
Yelagin Palace 123-5, 127
 Façade *125*
 Gardens and stables 123, *125*
 Oval Hall *124*
 Porcelain Room *123*, 125
Yurievskaya, Princess (Katya) 151, 153, 169

Zachery Constantinovich 87
Zacret House 118
Zemstov, Mikhail 183, *187*
Zubov, Platon 84, 86, 87, 114, 116